WITHDRAWN

TO HEAL
THE SCOURGE
OF PREJUDICE

TO HEAL
THE SCOURGE
OF PREJUDICE

The Life and Writings of
HOSEA EASTON

Edited with an Introduction by

GEORGE R. PRICE

and

JAMES BREWER STEWART

University of Massachusetts Press
Amherst

Introduction copyright © 1999 by
The University of Massachusetts Press
All rights reserved
Printed in the United States of America
LC 98-32262
ISBN 1-55849-184-8 (cloth); 185-6 (pbk.)
Designed by Jack Harrison
Set in Linotype Centennial by Keystone Typesetting, Inc.
Printed and bound by BookCrafters

Reprinted in this volume without significant editorial intervention are the
complete texts of the following works:

"An Address: Delivered before the Coloured Population, of Providence,
Rhode Island, on Thanksgiving Day, Nov. 27, 1828." By Hosea Easton, of
North Bridgewater, Mass. Boston: Printed by David Hooton, 152, Ann Street. 1828;

*A Treatise on the Intellectual Character, and Civil and Political Condition of the
Colored People of the U[nited] States; and the Prejudice Exercised towards Them:
With a Sermon on the Duty of the Church to Them.* By Rev. H. Easton,
a Colored Man. Boston: Printed and Published by Isaac Knapp. 1837.

Library of Congress Cataloging-in-Publication Data
Easton, H. (Hosea), b. 1787.
To heal the scourge of prejudice : the life and writings of
Hosea Easton / edited, with an introduction by George R. Price and
James Brewer Stewart.
p.   cm.
ISBN 1-55849-184-8 (cloth : alk. paper). —
ISBN 1-55849-185-6 (pbk. : alk. paper)
1. Afro-Americans—Social conditions—To 1964.
2. United States—Race relations.
3. Afro-Americans—Civil rights—History—19th century.
4. Racism—United States—History—19th century.
I. Price, George R. 1951–   . II. Stewart, James Brewer.
III Title.
E185.18.E27   1999
305.896′073—dc21   98-32262
CIP

British Library Cataloguing in Publication data are available.

*This book is published with the support and cooperation
of the University of Massachusetts Boston.*

To

Dickson D. Bruce

and

Kenneth A. Lockridge,

with thanks for getting us started.

CONTENTS

ACKNOWLEDGMENTS

The authors would like to thank the following individuals for their assistance in the preparation of this study: Bob Bigart, Dickson D. Bruce, Dorothy Carlson Stewart, Bruce Dain, Peter Drummey, Jane Emack-Cambra, Roy Finkenbine, Robert Forbes, Marie George, Robert Hall, Peter Hinks, James and Lois Horton, John Howe, David Ingram, Lorraine Kazhan, Michael Kuczkowski, Ella Kusnetz, Kenneth Lockridge, Michael Morrison, Matt Mulcahey, Gary B. Nash, Rich Newman, Millie Price, Patrick Rael, Calvin Roetzel, Athenaise Smith, Greta R. Smith, Kathryn Viens, Paul Wright, and Donald Yacovone. The staffs of the following libraries also furnished invaluable assistance: The Museum of African American History; African Meeting House; the Rhode Island Historical Society; the John Carter Brown Library; the New Bedford Public Library; the Old Colony Historical Society; the West Bridgewater Historical Society; the Massachusetts Historical Society; the Division of Manuscripts and Rare Books, Boston Public Library; the Family History Library; New England Genealogical and Historical Library; the Connecticut Historical Society; the Connecticut State Library; The Bienecke Library, Yale University.

TO HEAL
THE SCOURGE
OF PREJUDICE

INTRODUCTION

Hosea Easton and the Agony of Race

I. The Legacy of Hosea Easton

IN THE NORTH during the 1820s and 1830s, few became more deeply engaged in the struggles of free African Americans for equality than Hosea Easton. More important, no African American thinker of his era analyzed more systematically and cogently the deepest historical sources of racial injustice in the United States, the forces of white supremacy which have always made the struggle for black equality so difficult and so necessary. In the process, Easton raised fundamental questions which are as troubling today as they were when he first attacked them: Why do human beings possess different skin colors? What do these differences really mean? How does racial prejudice originate, and why is it so deeply embedded in American culture? How can a nation so devoted to equality oppress African Americans so systematically? In an environment of racial subordination, to what extent do black Americans remain connected to African origins and African history? To what degree have African Americans become like all other Americans, detached from their African antecedents? What has been the long-term impact of prejudice and exploitation on the intellectual, psychic, and cultural resources of African Americans? What can so oppressed a people do on their own to better themselves and their social conditions and to secure equality? What does the white majority owe African Americans as compensation to balance the scales of justice? How can the nightmare of racial domination and subordination truly be brought to an end?

Just before his death in 1837, Easton offered comprehensive answers to all these questions when he published *A Treatise on the Intellectual Character, and the Civil and Political Condition of the Colored People of the U[nited] States and the Prejudice Exercised towards Them,* the second of the two documents reproduced in this volume. Unprecedented for its analytical scope, biting social commentary, sweeping historical perspective, and outraged, impatient tone, the *Treatise* possesses unusual historical importance for several reasons. First, it vividly conveys the agonizing repression faced by African Americans in the antebellum North, their feelings of pain, anger, and frustration, and their optimistic faith that their persistence would ultimately "uplift" them to equality. Equally important, the *Treatise* reveals the thinking of an intelligent and perceptive leader as he struggled in a moment of deep crisis to provide new answers to problems facing the African American community and the nation as a whole. Finally, the content of Easton's ideas gives his *Treatise* a continuing pertinence, for it anticipates to a surprising degree the deep conflicts over "race" which currently set Americans so doggedly against one another. Such issues include: racial integration versus separatism; the existence of measurable biological differences between "races"; the validity of "Afrocentrism"; the justice of practicing "affirmative action" or granting "reparations"; the extent to which African American families and communities should be understood as having been damaged by deprivation and exploitation; and the impact of deprivation and discrimination on human development, beginning with the prenatal environment. Of course, Easton's treatment of these issues marks him as a product of the early nineteenth century, not as someone who anticipated our age. Nevertheless, the fact that he was the first American thinker to address all of these enduring questions in one comprehensive statement does have profound significance for us.

Easton's writings remind us forcefully that our present racial dilemmas are anything but unprecedented and that history affords us rich examples of people such as he who fused tenacity of will with the intellect and the moral vision to attack these problems creatively and comprehensively. In addition, Easton's *Treatise* documents the efforts of a committed activist to respond constructively to the fundamental crisis in northern race relations that overtook free African Americans during the 1820s and 1830s, a period as chaotic and threatening as any in which we have found ourselves. For African Americans of Easton's generation, the experience was agonizing, filled with racial tensions and exploding white violence that profoundly touched their collective self-understandings and their struggles for social justice.

The following sections of this introduction will outline the elements of this crisis, the events that set it in motion, and the nature of Hosea Easton's personal relationship to it. Only in these general contexts of social history and individual biography can the significance of Easton's understanding, and the profundity of his response, be appreciated fully. Knowledge of these matters should, in turn, prepare the reader to become engaged with the writings of Hosea Easton that have survived into our time, presented here in their original form.

II. The Making of Hosea Easton

In the memories of those who knew him, James Easton (1754–1830), Hosea Easton's father, was an extraordinary figure who exerted an enormous lifelong influence on his son. Though he was definitely of African ancestry and the grandson of slaves manumitted by Rhode Island Quakers at the turn of the eighteenth century, several gaps remain in James Easton's genealogy. He was born of free parents, probably of mixed lineage, near Middleborough, Massachusetts, where several generations of Wampanoag Indians and African Americans had often intermarried while living together in small villages, isolated by law from Middleborough's hostile whites. Evidence suggests, therefore that Easton was part Wampanoag and also part Narragan-

Easton Genealogy Chart

The Easton surname was first applied to Africans and Narragansett Indians through the son and grandson of Nicholas Easton, a Hutchinsonite exile from Massachusetts Bay Colony, who cofounded Newport, Rhode Island, in 1639. The Eastons became Quakers in the latter seventeenth century and freed their slaves during the 1690s. Those emancipated (but, as yet unidentified) Eastons eventually migrated to a Wampanoag village (probably Nemasket) just outside of Middleborough, Massachusetts, where James Easton was born.

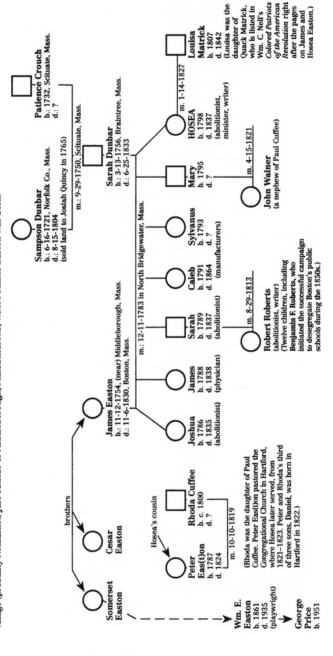

Sampson Dunbar
b.: 6-16-1721, Norfolk Co., Mass.
d.: 8-15-1804
(sold land to Josiah Quincy in 1765)

Patience Crouch
b.: 1732, Scituate, Mass.
d.: ?

m.: 9-29-1750, Scituate, Mass.

Sarah Dunbar
b.: 3-13-1756, Braintree, Mass.
d.: 6-25-1833

James Easton
b.: 11-12-1754, (near) Middleborough, Mass.
d.: 11-6-1830, Boston, Mass.

m.: 12-11-1783 in North Bridgewater, Mass.

brothers

Somerset Easton

Cesar Easton

Hosea's cousin

Peter East(l)on
b. 1787
d. 1824

Rhoda Cuffee
b. c. 1800
d. ?

m. 10-10-1819

(Rhoda was the daughter of Paul Cuffee. Peter East(l)on pastored the Congregational Church in Hartford, where Hosea later served, from 1821–1823. Peter and Rhoda's third of three sons, Daniel, was born in Hartford in 1822.)

Wm. E. Easton
b. 1861
d. 1935
(playwright)

George Price
b. 1951

Joshua
b. 1786
d. 1835
(abolitionist)

James
b. 1788
d. 1838
(physician)

Sarah
b. 1789
d. 1837
(abolitionist)

m. 8-29-1813

Robert Roberts
(abolitionist, writer)
(Twelve children, including Benjamin F. Roberts, who initiated the successful campaign to desegregate Boston's public schools during the 1850s.)

Caleb
b. 1791
d. 1864

Sylvanus
b. 1793
d. ?
(manufacturers)

Mary
b. 1795
d. ?

m. 4-15-1821

John Wainer
(a nephew of Paul Cuffee)

HOSEA
b. 1798
d. 1837
(abolitionist, minister, writer)

m. 1-14-1827

Louisa Matrick
b. 1807
d. 1842
(Louisa was the daughter of Quack Matrick, who is listed in Wm. C. Nell's *Colored Patriots of the American Revolution* right after the pages on James and Hosea Easton.)

{ 4 }

sett. Historical records and documents refer to him as either "black" or "colored," the common terms in colonial and early republic records for people of color, no matter what their actual ancestry may have been.

Like so many people with such a multiracial inheritance, James Easton embraced the patriotic cause, seeing in the American Revolution the promise of equal citizenship. He served under George Washington as a fortifications engineer. In 1780 he left his Wampanaoag neighbors, seeking the opportunities of capitalism that citizens had always enjoyed but from which indigenous people had been customarily and legislatively excluded. He settled in North Bridgewater (now Brockton, Massachusetts), a town with very few residents of color, married in 1783, and took up the skilled craft of ironworking as his profession. James Easton's wife, Sarah, was the daughter of Sampson Dunbar, a respected citizen of Braintree and later of Stoughton, Massachusetts. In most civil records Sampson Dunbar is referred to as a "mulatto," but in others he receives no racial designation, suggesting that some local clerks possibly regarded him as "white." James and Sarah Easton had seven children between the years of 1786 and 1799: five sons and two daughters. Hosea was the youngest, born 1 September 1798.

With "black, "red," and "white" so commingled in the family history, it is not surprising that one of James's sons, Caleb, married into one of North Bridgewater's more distinguished white families, or that Hosea would one day declare that all humanity, whatever the skin color, was united in "one blood." To the Eastons, as to so many people of color (and some whites) in the earliest years of the republic, rigid racial distinctions between "black," "white," and "red" conflicted fundamentally with personal experience.[1]

As an ironworker, James Easton specialized in edge tools, farm implements, and sea chain and anchors. He also produced industrial iron used in the large building projects he supervised, such as the construction of Boston's Tremont Theater and the laying of track for the Boston Marine Railway. Clearly he was as much a contractor as an artisan, and one senses that he had the dignified bearing of a gentleman, at ease in the commercial culture of eastern Massachusetts that blossomed at the conclusion of the War of 1812. "He was welcome in the business circles of Boston as a man of strict integrity," recalled the historian and Easton contemporary, William Cooper Nell, and "the many who sought his advice on complicated matters styled him 'the Black lawyer.' " His rise had been truly impressive.[2]

Protective of his hard-won position, James Easton met bigotry with defiant assertions of equality. When the Eastons' church constructed a "negro porch," for instance, the family remained resolutely seated on the main floor. Finally, exasperated whites had to eject them bodily. On another occasion, the family purchased a pew in a Baptist church. When white parishioners coated it with tar, the Eastons, uncowed and defiant, arrived the following Sunday carrying seats of their own. When the laity prevented them from setting up their chairs, the family refused to move. They returned weekly until formal banishment forced them out. The impact of confrontations such as these on young Hosea must have been profound, and permanent.[3]

As these incidents also make clear, the Easton name carried serious obligations, which many of James's descendants discharged with distinction. In the next generation, a total of five sons, daughters, and their spouses became abolitionists. The oldest son, Joshua, was active in the National Colored Convention movement and was selected by the Massachusetts General Colored Association to be their representative in 1833 to the first annual meeting of the New England Anti-Slavery Society. Daughter Sarah, who married the prominent Boston black abolitionist Robert Roberts, was eulogized for her own activism in William Lloyd Garrison's *Liberator* when she died in 1837. (Sarah died exactly one week after Hosea, who was also eulogized in the *Liberator.*) Her son, Benjamin F. Roberts, initiated in 1849 a famous Boston desegregation case which foreshadowed the 1954 United States Supreme Court decision forcing the integration of the nation's public schools. Two more of James Easton's grandchildren fought in the Civil War, and another descendant, William Edgar Eas-

{ 6 }

ton, became an activist playwright following a post–Civil War career in Texas Republican Party politics.[4]

James Easton's patriarchical stature, personal tenacity, and unquestioned "respectability" marked him as a member of an African American elite that rose to prominence just after the Revolution, even as northern slavery was still in the process of being dismantled. Civic-minded businessmen, clergymen, and educators such as Philadelphia's James Forten, Boston's Prince Hall, and New York City's John Teasman perpetuated values of self-improvement while leading initial efforts to found the churches, schools, fraternal orders, and voluntary associations that initially solidified free black urban communities. From the late eighteenth century onward, these men were unremitting in their efforts to secure racial equality and self-respect by putting the values of "uplift" into practice. Leaders of ambition, ability, and vision (men like James Easton), were constantly exhorted to impart to those who followed them their own values of temperance, piety, thrift, self-control, and above all, education.[5]

In providing this style of leadership, James Easton and these other patriarchal figures demonstrated their belief that the African American community positioned itself along a moral continuum of observable personal qualities, with "degradation" defining the negative pole and "respectability" the positive. According to a hierarchy of personal virtue, those who were defeated by the devastating impact of slavery and discrimination occupied the lower ranks, while those who exerted their free will for the sake of self-improvement, community strength, and racial equality occupied the higher ones. It was an ideology well suited to meet the principal challenge of James Easton's era—the development of stable African American communities out of the disparate populations of urbanized free blacks, culturally assimilated Indians, escapees from southern slavery, and immigrants from the French and British Caribbean who arrived soon after the Revolution.[6]

Behind the concept of personal "uplift" lay the seldom-questioned assumption that in order to achieve equality mixed people of color must subdue their cultural distinctiveness to conform to Anglo-

American norms. This effort required them to turn away from distinctive ethnic customs whose roots were in African and Native American cultures. Most New Englanders who remained categorized as Native Americans, by contrast, generally showed scant interest in adapting to the dominant patterns of Anglo-American life. To them, "uplift" recalled all too vividly the oppressive "praying towns," territorial dispossession, and economic dependency to which Anglo-Americans had for so long subjected them. They elected, therefore, to preserve their traditions even as, ironically, many elements of both Native American and African American culture were already becoming interwoven throughout Anglo-American life, particularly foods, medicines, music, sports, and linguistic patterns, significant contributions which have been recognized only recently.[7] But "uplift-minded" colored Americans who were determined to face the world culturally as "black people" defined themselves just as James Easton did—as Protestant in religion, capitalist in their economic assumptions, and patriotic "republican" in their political values, with social progress measured by the pace of their social and economic inclusion in American society. Partly for this reason, the proposal that African Americans be "returned" to West Africa became increasingly abhorrent to northern free blacks as the nineteenth century opened.

The powerful credo of "uplift," however, registered deeply within James Easton's family and was particularly influential in young Hosea's upbringing. Above all, the idea inspired a startling experiment in "uplift" undertaken by James Easton beginning in the second decade of the nineteenth century. His decision to incorporate into his family's iron foundry a manual labor school for promising "colored youth" bespeaks uncommon self-confidence and imagination. Unprecedented in the annals of African American history and the history of American education, this visionary experiment implanted values of "respectability" in the young Hosea Easton as nothing else could have.[8]

The school addressed the problem of underemployment among young male African Americans. Twenty boys were supported each year as student-laborers in the Easton foundry, dividing their time between academic study and vocational training in smithing, farming, and shoemaking. At every turn, James and his fellow teachers imparted values of "respectability," and Hosea, now in his teens, proved an enthusiastic participant. Stern moral codes and "rigid economy" were enforced with "surprising assiduity," he recalled, and "ardent spirits found no place in the establishment." Yet for all their effort, and despite the "many thousands of dollars" invested by James and his partners, the school closed after perhaps a decade. According to James's grandson Benjamin Roberts, the "prejudice of the community and the unpopularity of the enterprise" finally overwhelmed its finances.[9] Hosea Easton likewise blamed prejudice, but in far more bitter terms in the *Treatise:*

> By reason of the repeated surges of the tide of prejudice, the establishment, like a ship in a boisterous hurricane at sea, went beneath its waves richly laden, well manned, and well managed, and all sunk to rise no more. . . . It fell, and with it fell the hearts of several of its undertakers in despair, and their bodies into their graves.

As this passage implies, James Easton's death in Boston in 1830 probably followed soon after the collapse of his business and educational ventures. At about the same time, Hosea Easton, his wife Louisa, and their two young children moved to Boston, also suggesting that the manual labor school expired toward the end of the 1820s. Those Easton family members who remained in North Bridgewater rapidly moved into shoemaking, the specialty of the next generation. But the "master spirits and high minds" that Hosea Easton so admired during his years at the school, and, most of all, the example of James Easton, led him to adopt a different course. Though one day he would lament the failure of his father's dreams, he first made them his own by preparing for the ministry. And though the historical record is silent concerning those years of preparation, by 1828 he clearly had come far.

March of that year found him in Boston, chairing a "large and respectable meeting of the People of Color" in support of *Freedom's Journal,* the nation's only newspaper published by African Americans. In June, Boston's black Methodists charged him to raise funds to pay off the mortgage on their recently constructed meeting house. In November, 1828, he delivered a powerful and revealing "Thanksgiving Day Address" to the "Coloured Population" of Providence, Rhode Island, the other document reprinted in this volume. Hosea Easton now moved, as his father had, among the elite leaders of the African American community.[10]

III. The Racial Crisis of the 1820s

When Hosea Easton spoke in Providence in 1828, he did so not only as the voice of a deeply aggrieved community, but also as a bringer of God's liberating promise of equality through "uplift." In discharging this responsibility, he called forth powerful feelings of intensely focused anger accompanied by a vibrant message of hope. This, of course, had also been his father's twofold approach when passionately defying white bigots while at the same time striving to "uplift" the young. Because of this balancing of anger with Christian hope, readers will find that in the "Thanksgiving Address" extraordinarily vivid expressions of rage against white oppressors exist as a counterpoint to, and are ultimately overcome by, providential assurances of black "uplift" and liberation. Messages of Christian redemption and condemnation of the almost unspeakable evils involved in slaveholding—atrocities such as rape, forced abortion, mutilation, starvation, and murder—play against one another throughout the "Address" before being finally swept away by prophecies of spiritual transformation and racial equality. It is hard to imagine a historical document that captures more fully the complexity and power of the ideology of African American "uplift" or the extraordinary effect of its message upon black communities in their day-to-day struggles to improve themselves.[11]

The "Address" also conveys Easton's continuing reliance on his father as a model of inspiration and on ingrained family traditions. When, for example, he invokes "brave Washington" and his "valiant confederates" for their defenses of liberty, and when he sings "anthems of praise to God for rearing us from nothing into a great and mighty nation," he is clearly transmuting his patriot-father's revolutionary achievements into his own theology of divinely guided progress. And when he addresses the problem of racial discrimination in the North, Easton again registers powerful memories of his father when lamenting that free blacks everywhere were exiled from politics, deprived of schooling, barred from "respectable" businesses, and driven into "immorality." Even when African Americans were properly educated, he complains, the heightened ambitions and expectations of their young people, when thwarted by the barriers and limitations placed in front of them by racism, only led them more rapidly to blasted hopes and "relapse into sordid dissipation." It was exactly this problem that James Easton had tried to address in his manual labor school. Finally, Easton also suggests in this "Address" just how deeply wounded he felt by every one of his humiliating encounters with prejudiced whites. Justly proud of his noteworthy attainments as a "respectable" man of God, he felt that every such incident constituted a nearly unspeakable assault on his personal dignity, his sense of self-worth, and even on his very "manhood." It distressed and embittered him, he all but admits, to be forced to share segregated quarters with "tavern haunters and drunkards" or to be escorted by the white minister to "some remote part of the Meeting-House, or . . . a box built above the gallery."

As the 1828 "Address" suggests, then, Hosea Easton's passion for "uplift" derived, in part, from a deeply personal commitment to uphold his family's honor and to preserve his own. He consequently placed enormous expectations on himself and on "uplifted" African Americans generally to gain equality and redeem their nation's promises of liberty. By "uplifting" themselves by dint of their own efforts, African Americans would also be acting to advance racial equality in the United States at large.

Introduction

As his heated condemnations of white prejudice make clear, Easton harbored no illusions either that "uplift" could be achieved with ease or that whites would abandon their prejudices readily. He certainly was aware that as the 1820s wore on, whites in the North rapidly were becoming more overtly hostile toward African Americans, more eager to provoke violence, and increasingly better organized for expressing their racial hatreds. In response, as Easton also knew, ordinary free blacks were growing more defensive and militant as well, while among the black elite disagreements multiplied as to whether the goal of racial equality was even conceivable in the United States. As the 1820s ran their course, race relations throughout the North began building toward crisis.

Many converging historical trends contributed to this process. As urban life in the North underwent greater social differentiation, troubling new divisions of class and color increasingly became apparent to practically everyone. As a result, racial tensions multiplied. Lower-class white men, for example, had always been drawn to African American bars, bordellos, music houses, and theaters—enterprises that Hosea Easton had in mind in his 1828 "Address" when he condemned "degraded" behavior within the black community. Now, however, these whites exhibited new feelings of hostility even as they flocked to black-faced minstrel shows, patronized black-run houses of prostitution, applauded black entertainers, and tossed down drinks in black speakeasies. When first encountering the traumas of industrial wage labor, these ordinary whites, most of them immigrants, saw in the "blackness" of their African American neighbors not only unwelcome competition in a tightening labor market, but also a mirror of their diminishing sense of self-worth. Irish and non–Anglo-Saxon European immigrants to America were made to feel inferior to the older, more firmly established Anglo-American families. The immigrants were at a competitive disadvantage in their new world, where the focus was placed on their "differentness." But when they could turn the social focus to their shared "whiteness," they found an opportunity to place themselves on a rung of the American social ladder that was at least higher than the one occupied by persons of color. Thus the impulse to assert one's "whiteness" and personal value by committing violence against black people grew ever stronger and more widespread.[12]

In response, African American working people turned their traditional public gatherings, first begun in the 1790s to commemorate northern emancipation and Haiti's black revolution, into militant mass marches featuring uniformed companies complete with swords and arms. These events, organized after whites had begun expelling African Americans from local militia parades, highlighted the black communities' abolitionist feelings and powers of mobilization. In response, nervous whites satirized these gatherings by circulating white supremacist handbills which conveyed their resentment of self-assured black people who insisted that the streets belonged to them as much as to anyone. Thus even those landmarks of "uplift" that bespoke the black elites' greatest successes now contributed to growing racial tension. Handsome brick churches, meeting halls, and school buildings confirmed to everyone that African Americans had powerful leaders, financial resources, and a will to strengthen their communal ties. In every northern city, African American sabbath observances and school day activities fell victim to periodic white harassment. While residing in Boston from 1829 to 1833, Hosea Easton was certainly close to all these developments.[13]

Meanwhile, in Easton's Massachusetts as in many other northern states, politicians voted their growing prejudices, and urban whites took them into the streets. Legislatures in newly admitted western states wrote constitutions that denied African Americans basic civil rights, and the Massachusetts state legislature came close to emulating them in 1821. That same year, the newly ratified New York State constitution stripped African American men worth less than $250 in personal property of their right to vote. Urban white racial violence also began to intensify. During the mid- and late 1820s, mob activity directed against black communities flared in several northern cities, Boston included, and in 1829 mobs in Cincinnati used unprecedented terrorism to force several hundred African Americans into exile in Canada. Soon after, President Andrew Jackson informed the Cherokee Nation (probably the American Indian tribe of that era most successfully acculturated to dominant white norms) that no amount of adaptation on their part would prevent their expulsion from lands in Georgia, Alabama, Tennessee, and North Carolina sought by slave owners and gold seekers. The attribute of "whiteness," it seemed, was mandatory in order to live unchallenged on American soil. The multiple tragedies inherent in this trend surely did not escape Hosea Easton, who traced his lineage to forebears who were "white" as well as "black" and "red."[14]

From African Americans' perspectives, however, the greatest threat of racial expulsion came neither from mobs nor from the president, but from the American Colonization Society, which rapidly expanded its influence in the late 1820s. As racial tension increased, so did the society's budget, number of local affiliates, and endorsements by leading politicians and ministers. To some colonizationists, sponsoring the voluntary repatriation of free blacks to West Africa was a humanitarian project. It encouraged private emancipations by slaveholders and the Christianization of Africa by "uplifted," intelligent blacks who had wisely removed themselves from the grip of white prejudice. To other members of the society, particularly politicians in northern cities and planters across the South, colonization offered the promise of reducing the growing population of free blacks who were deemed "dangerous" subverters of the stability of slavery and unwelcome competitors to white wage laborers.[15]

To African American critics, however, such distinctions in motive were meaningless. To them, the eminent jurists, ministers, and politicians who led the Colonization Society cloaked malevolent intentions in a false "benevolence," seeking to perpetuate slavery by driving free African Americans into exile. To claim, as some colonizationists did, that black people possessed the admirable capacity to "uplift" themselves but should depart from the United States nevertheless struck African American critics as rank hypocrisy. Easton repeated the essence of this generally held opinion when he condemned the society in the 1828 "Address" as a "diabolical pursuit." "They will steal the sons of Africa," he exclaimed, "bring them to America, keep them and their posterity in bondage for centuries, . . . then transport them back to Africa by which means America gets all her drudgery done at little expense." "They will meet the God of justice," Easton prophesied, "which to them will be a devouring sword." Easton's militant friend, David Walker, commented no less angrily in his famous 1829 *Appeal . . . to the Coloured Citizens of the World:* "Do they think they can bundle us up like brutes and send us off as they did to the brethren of the state of Ohio?" Walker, of course, was referring to the bloodbath in Cincinnati that had forced over a thousand free blacks into exile.[16]

As Walker's harsh tone suggests, new strains of anger and alienation were appearing in the pronouncements of the elite. In the face of a compounding racial crisis, the continuing efficacy of "uplift," as preached by leaders like Hosea Easton, was certainly open to question. In his *Appeal,* Walker called not only for spiritual transformation, but also for the appropriate use of violence in defense of black freedom. Some other influential representatives of the African American elite displayed similar doubts as they explored nationalist and separatist ways of thinking, particularly the idea that black Americans should embrace their cultural connections with the glories of ancient Egypt and sub-Saharan Africa or perhaps immigrate to Haiti, an Afro-Caribbean culture presumably superior to that of the white United States.[17]

Seeking to heal their internal divisions in the face of impending crisis, the elites of New York City, Philadelphia, Boston, and several smaller cities announced the formation of a new and unprecedented organization, the National Colored Convention, designed to link and unite the efforts of black leaders in every major population center. When it assembled in Philadelphia in 1831, delegates from a dozen cities and towns were in attendance, composing an impressive cross section of black leadership throughout the North. In response to the terrifying Cincinnati riots, its principal order of business was to debate the feasibility of voluntary immigration to Canada. The long quest to attain equality by pursuing "uplift" within the United States had clearly reached a dangerous impasse.[18]

IV. The Triumph of "Whiteness," 1831–1837

At this gathering, and in subsequent meetings of the National Colored Convention, Hosea Easton played a prominent role as one of Boston's four representatives. While mingling with powerful apostles of "uplift" from his father's generation as well as with many young activists like himself, he served as chaplain and often led the assembly in prayer. He also offered well-received resolutions and served on committees that promoted anticolonization and "uplift." Following adjournments, he continued to discharge his convention responsibilities back in Boston by convening protest meetings against the American Colonization Society and organizing various fund-raising efforts.

One project undertaken by the initial meeting of the convention, however, captured Easton's attention as no other could. Three radical white abolitionists appeared at this 1831 gathering to propose the establishment of a manual labor college for young African American men, to be located in New Haven, Connecticut. One can only imagine the range of Easton's reactions when Arthur Tappan, Simeon Jocelyn, and William Lloyd Garrison, religious visionaries dedicated to eradicating the sins of racial oppression, promised ten thousand dollars toward the development of such an institution. Members of the convention, however, were required to raise matching funds. Suddenly, as Easton understood it, these daring white reformers actually were proposing to help revive his recently deceased father's visionary project, but on a scale much larger than even James Easton had attempted. As Jocelyn, Garrison, and Tappan described their proposal, the school was planned to attract not only talented young men from all over New England, but also the sons of wealthy free black trading families from Barbados and Jamaica, since New Haven had such close commercial ties to the Caribbean. The presence of nearby Yale

University, they emphasized, was expected to add intellectual luster to the endeavor.[19]

In making this bold proposal, Garrison, Tappan, and Jocelyn were acting as leaders of a new and unprecedented radical white abolitionist movement which had burst forth in 1831 around the time of the convention and which would continue its work until well after the Civil War. Believing slaveholding to be the most heinous of all sins, each of these men, like all the new white abolitionists, embraced the doctrine of "immediate abolition," the idea that all slaves must be granted their freedom without delay. They also endorsed the doctrine of African American and white equality, a conviction that would be self-evident especially after black people had been given the means to improve themselves intellectually and morally by practicing "uplift" and achieving "respectability." The idea of founding a manual labor college in New Haven seemed a perfect way to put such beliefs into action, especially since such an assertion of black equality reinforced recent decisions by all three white abolitionists to resign in angry protest from the American Colonization Society. This action, if nothing else, assured them a respectful hearing by the National Colored Convention.[20]

Once Garrison and his colleagues had finished their presentation, the delegates gave the college project a unanimous endorsement. Easton joined many others in volunteering for fund raising, and he then returned to Boston, eager to make his father's dreams live again. This project, surely, was a powerful confirmation of his prophetic belief that God stood ready to redeem the black community. But like the others at the convention, Easton also embraced the proposal for a manual labor college as a way to break the impasse facing the elite. By working with whites like Garrison and Tappan to realize such plans, he and the other black leaders would not only overcome their defensiveness and inner doubts concerning aggressive new postures against their multiplying white antagonists, but they also would progress toward the goal of uniting their communities to secure "respectable" futures. With the support of their new white allies, the black leaders quickly began to sponsor a profusion of new projects on behalf of "uplift," of which the manual labor college was only one. Sabbath schools, debating and literary societies, "moral improvement" clubs, choral groups, and temperance organizations began springing up in towns and cities across the North.[21]

But when set in the context of the compounding racial crisis of the 1820s, the disruptive potential of a biracial movement for immediate abolition is nearly impossible to calculate. Never before in the history of the free states had relations between people of different skin colors become more volatile as lower-class white bullies joined "respectable" colonizationists in opposing the efforts of free African Americans. Never before had white violence flared so intensely in northern cities, had the American Colonization Society acted so aggressively, or had white politicians (in the Jacksonian spirit) legislated their prejudices so heavily. Never before had the black elites themselves faced such impatient criticism from voices within their own communities, such divided understandings of their place as "Americans," or such uncertainty about the efficacy of their own efforts. Never before, in short, had disagreements in the North over the meaning of "race" carried such explosive potential. When figures such as William Lloyd Garrison and Hosea Easton insisted that members of both races must collaborate in a crusade for black equality through the attainment of "respectability," they inadvertently ignited a racial explosion of unprecedented scope among bigoted whites, for their programs of "uplift" magnified tremendously all of the racial tensions that had been multiplying in the North throughout the 1820s.

What followed, therefore, was not the fulfillment of Easton's vision of racial redemption, but disaster. Seldom in the nation's history has there been so striking an example of reformers' long-term intentions being overwhelmed by the unintended consequences of their initial acts. As William Lloyd Garrison and Hosea Easton embraced a program of "uplift" that they believed ultimately would benefit all the races, they found themselves reviled throughout the North as race mixing subversives in a conspiracy to challenge the sanctity and social advantage of "whiteness." When the news broke in New Haven that African American students were soon to arrive in the city, whites of all classes, "respectable" colonizationists as well as ordinary wage laborers, reacted swiftly in a united program of racial terrorism. While one mob pelted Arthur Tappan's home with garbage, another invaded "New Liberia," as whites termed New Haven's lower-class black enclave, to vent their wrath. Colonizationists, meanwhile, condemned the abolitionists for "firebrand" behavior and recommended that free blacks consider removing themselves to the "peaceful havens" of West Africa. But the common goal of both white groups was to force reformers of different skin colors to abandon the project of "raising" African Americans to "respectable" stations equal to their own. Their harsh messages enforced an unvarying political axiom that presumed biological truths: black and white had always been distinct races and must live forever separately and unequally. As events in New Haven made clear, well before the abolitionists had created even the semblance of a national organization, their crusade was being systematically suppressed.[22]

Over the next several years, as towns and cities across the Northeast exploded in violence that repeated New Haven's example, the spreading pattern confirmed to everyone that the abolitionists' interracial crusade was being crushed at its inception. The vision of an American society open to African Americans who could be inspired to "rise" to equality was being obliterated. In its place was emerging a rigidly racialized system in which discriminatory distinctions on the basis of skin color alone would determine human relations. This was the lesson learned by Prudence Crandall and her supporters in 1832, when threatening mobs and colonizationist politicians practicing legislative intimidation thwarted her attempt to open an integrated school for girls in Canterbury, Connecticut. The lesson was learned again in that same year, when mobs destroyed the racially integrated, abolitionist-sponsored Noyes Academy in Dover, New Hampshire, and in 1834–35, when white violence in Cincinnati greeted attempts of white abolitionists to offer private schooling to African Americans.

A DECLARATION

OF THE SENTIMENTS OF THE PEOPLE OF HARTFORD, REGARDING THE MEASURES

OF THE

Abolitionists.

CONSIDERING that it is no less the *duty* than the right of freemen, to express their sentiments on all questions materially affecting the prosperity of the country or the maintenance of its liberties and free institutions; and regarding the moral force of public opinion as the basis and primary elemental principle of our government, *the Citizens of Hartford* cannot view with indifference the excitement which now prevails on the subject of slavery in the United States.

This excitement has been occasioned by the rash and reckless measures and proceedings of the Abolitionists of the Middle and Northern States. We believe that these proceedings will result in no good, but much evil; that their direct and obvious tendency is to agitate and alarm the people of the slave States; endanger their peace and security, if not expose them to the evils and horrors of insurrection, massacre and a servile war—to injure the slave population and subject them to restrictions and severities from which they have hitherto been exempt, and greatly defer, if not wholly extinguish the hope of the final amelioration of their condition—that they tend to destroy that reciprocal harmony and confidence which should prevail among the people of different sections of the Union; to embarrass commercial and social intercourse among them, to alienate their minds and to "weaken those sacred ties which hold together its several parts."

And furthermore, we believe, and declare, that the conduct of the Abolitionists, in distributing their incendiary publications—not discussing the subject of slavery, but addressed only to the passions of a degraded and servile population —in the slave holding States, in violation of their laws and in contravention of the spirit of the constitution of the United States, which guarantees to each State the exclusive regulation of all local interests, including that of master and slave, is wholly unjustifiable—a contempt of public opinion, a flagrant outrage against the society which affords them protection, and a high *offence* against the *principles of morality*, because their whole conduct is predicated on a total recklessness of consequences, which can only proceed from depravity of heart or desperate infatuation.

With these views of the subject, we declare our solemn conviction, that it is the duty of all good citizens, by word, deed and example, to condemn and discountenance the violent measures of the Abolitionists, and to use all reasonable and peaceable means, consistent with their own rights, to put an end to them; to restore quiet to the public mind, and harmony and confidence among the people of every section of our happy confederacy.

HARTFORD, OCTOBER, 1835.

Anonymous antiabolitionist declaration from 1835, during Hosea Easton's tenure as pastor of Hartford's Talcott Street Congregational Church. It is not clear whether this unsigned document was meant to be a petition, a newspaper notice, or a handbill. *Courtesy of the Connecticut Historical Society, Hartford, Connecticut.*

White race riots swept through Boston, New York City, Hartford, Pitts-burgh, and Utica, New York, during 1834, 1835, and 1836, intimidat-ing abolitionists and leaving the dream of equality through "uplift" buried under the smoking rubble of African Americans' churches and private homes.[23]

As violence mounted, the behavior of white abolitionists also changed in ways that undermined the interracial coalition. When Garrison toured England in 1833, his way was paid by free blacks who had commissioned him to raise funds for the manual labor col-lege. He returned empty handed and full of weak excuses, as though his determination, as well as his mission, had suffered defeat. In re-sponse to the mobs, meetings of the antislavery societies issued hand-bills and resolutions denying any intention to promote the "mixing" of races. White reformers became divided over the appropriateness of sponsoring racially integrated schools as opposed to independent black schools and colleges and differed over the possibility of found-ing an abolitionist political party; to these debates were added other controversies about the truth of various complex religious doctrines and the problem of male dominance within the abolitionist move-ment. Although some of these issues were tangential to African Amer-ican interests, they were all indicative of the white abolitionists' at-tempts to respond with new approaches to the violence that had crushed their initial crusade. By the time a white mob had reduced Philadelphia's Free Speech Hall to ashes in 1838, white abolitionists were divided among themselves and Hosea Easton had been dead for almost a year. But his belief in the egalitarian power of racial "uplift" had expired earlier still.[24]

The process had begun, of course, with the collapse of the Easton family's foundry and school in the late 1820s and with James Easton's death soon thereafter. In 1833, however, when Hosea Easton became the pastor of the Talcott Street Congregational Church in Hartford, Connecticut, where racial tensions ran unusually high, his beliefs in the power of "uplift" were so severely tested that they ultimately proved impossible to sustain. In January 1834, for example, Easton agreed to raise funds for the Hartford Literary and Religious Institution, which he and others had founded to foster piety and respectability. Soon after, white mobsters attacked one of his parishioners just after he had left church. Three days of rioting followed, punctuated by gunfire from an African American resister. In the aftermath, several black families found themselves homeless, thanks to the depredations of roving white mobs, and the Literary and Religious Institution decided to relieve Easton of his fund-raising responsibilities. "We are sorry to say," its corresponding secretary reported, "that in consequence of the . . . mobocracy that prevailed before our agent could be properly introduced before the public . . . we felt it best to call him home." The son of the defiant James Easton had now been silenced and his "uplift" project stifled.[25]

Henceforth, Easton and his parishioners lived in periodic terror of their white neighbors. In the space of three years, from 1834 through 1836, mobs attacked them on at least three occasions. Street corner harassment was constant. In June 1835, the worst violence of all exploded just outside Easton's Talcott Street Church when white harassers again provoked a black resister to take up arms. Three days of rioting followed, and neither the local police nor the militia could save black neighborhoods from looters and vandals. After touring the United States during the mid-1830s, the English observer Edward Abdy remarked that never in all his travels had he seen such systematic brutality as that which he witnessed daily in Hartford:

> Throughout the Union, there is, perhaps, no city, containing the same amount of population, where the blacks meet with more contumely and unkindness than at this place. Some of them told me it was hardly safe for them to be in the streets alone at night. . . . To pelt them with stones, and cry out nigger! nigger! as they pass, seems to be the pastime of the place.

In Hartford, as everywhere else, the dream of securing black equality through "uplift" died violently and quickly.[26]

Then, in 1836, Easton's church burned to the ground.[27] He had just

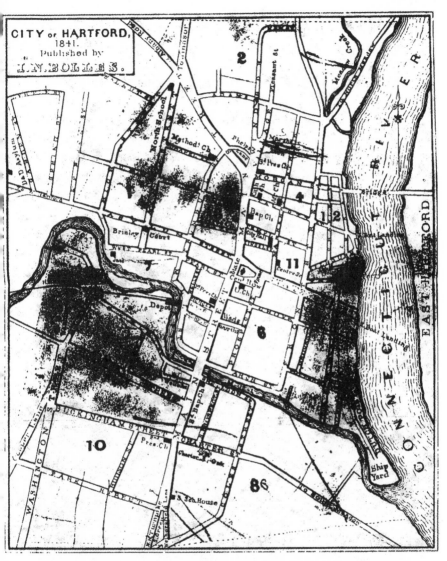

Map of Hartford, 1841. The Talcott Street Congregational Church that Hosea Easton pastored is designated here as "Afr. Ch." and is located in the fourth district. The Colored Methodist Episcopal Zion Church that Easton founded is not shown here since it burned down in 1836 and was not rebuilt until 1842. From *Martinson's New Directory and Guidebook for the City of Hartford,* compiled by Isaac N. Bolles, 1841.

taken over the pastorship of the new Colored Methodist Episcopal Zion Church that year, and though the cause of the fire remains unexplained, the devastating impact on Easton quickly became evident. Spring 1837 found him speaking far from home, in places such as Mansfield, Massachusetts, and Dover, New Hampshire, soliciting funds with which to rebuild. His reported remarks document the depth of his despair and his comprehensive effort to reformulate his understanding of the problem of "race." He now concluded that equality achieved through black "uplift" could not succeed in a white-dominated society that crushed every initiative and visited terror and destruction on innocent African Americans. "Methinks were I one of that people," mused one of Easton's white listeners, "I would turn my back on a land where so many obstacles lie in the way of their elevation."[28] As this terrible reality took hold, Easton felt compelled to explain to himself and to anyone willing to listen why his life's work had

The Colored Methodist Episcopal Zion Church, 1842–1856, to which Easton's congregation moved after the fire of 1836 destroyed the church at its original location. In 1856 the church changed its name to the African Methodist Episcopal Zion Church and moved to Pearl Street, where it remained until 1898. *Courtesy of the Harriet Beecher Stowe Center, Hartford, Connecticut.*

proved unavailing and what new approaches could be constructed in its place. Four months before his death he published his conclusions. In the *Liberator* of 13 March, he advertised his *Treatise on the Intellectual Character, and the Civil and Political Condition of the Colored People of the U[nited] States* as a work that, "rolls up the curtain, and introduces the reader to those colored American citizens who have been for so long despised and almost unknown."[29]

In writing this *Treatise,* the disillusioned Easton retained far less interest in preaching to African Americans than he had shown in his 1828 "Address." Instead, he spoke almost exclusively to whites, challenging them, first, to understand the enormity of their transgressions, and second, to make haste to redress them. Reports of public lectures he delivered just before his death confirm that Easton now regarded himself as a missionary to the "unredeemed" whites, who must be inspired to "uplift" themselves from their condition of bigoted, exploitative savagery.

V. Easton's *Treatise* and the Agony of Race

As the *Treatise* makes clear from the beginning, Easton wished to demonstrate conclusively that African American "uplift" offered no solution for racial oppression. Instead, whites must be made to understand just how deeply rooted in their history and culture their crimes against dark-skinned people actually were. Then, perhaps, they would begin to realize how unjust and impossible it was to expect black Americans to prove their "fitness" for equality by "improving" themselves. If whites could instead be made to take responsibility for their actions, it would then be possible, Easton reasoned, for them to take it upon themselves to end the agony of race. Yet as harshly as he censored white Americans throughout the *Treatise,* he also prayed for his oppressor's redemption. His only alternative, to plan for their physical overthrow, was not only patently impossible, but also contradicted all his Christian values.[30]

However we might evaluate his reasoning, Easton's analysis

clearly merits our attention for its scope and depth of insight and for its unsparing honesty. Few statements from the pre–Civil War era convey more fully the anguish of living moment-to-moment in a world of prejudice or describe in more compelling detail its ordinary manifestations. Easton also deserves recognition for his intellectual courage. Before his *Treatise,* no American writer had ever attempted so comprehensive an analysis of "black and white" in all of its ramifications. No one of his time, moreover, presents a more compelling example than does Easton of an individual responding to personal anguish by reflecting anew on the very problems that so beleaguered him, his community, and the nation at large. As a morally engaged thinker responding intelligently to a profound moment of crisis, Hosea Easton had few peers.[31]

Despite his originality, however, Easton worked his arguments around facts and ideas that circulated widely in his day. The *Treatise* is therefore significant for its analytical scope and expressive power, not because of the raw material from which it was fashioned. This becomes clear in the Introduction, in which Easton connects two central contentions that inform the work as a whole: first, that people of every skin color share a single God-created essence and therefore "one blood"; and second, that racial distinctions between African Americans and whites first took root in biblical times, when some of Noah's descendants created advanced societies in Africa while others migrated to Europe and degenerated into savagery.

The first idea was drawn from Christian environmentalism, which had undergirded the African American case for equality from the very beginning. In the eighteenth century, abolitionist-minded evangelical Quakers and rationalists such as Benjamin Franklin had embraced this notion, as had revolutionary-era black patriarchs such as James Easton. To abolitionists of the 1820s and 1830s, Christian environmentalism constituted an unquestioned article of faith, and in his *Appeal,* David Walker had transformed it into a revolutionary principle. Even certain colonizationists took an environmentalist view of race, arguing that though African Americans were potentially the equals of whites, unchangeable prejudice in the United States doomed their efforts to "rise" and left them no alternative but to return to the welcoming culture of Africa. Whatever their diverse conclusions, however, all of these individuals believed, much as Hosea Easton emphasized throughout the *Treatise,* that observable human differences like skin color were superficial accidents of nature, never to be confused with the uniform, underlying equality of God's human creation. All agreed that if black people could be liberated from oppressive circumstances imposed on them by whites, their fundamental equality with all other humans would become undeniable.[32]

The second major contention of the Introduction was also derived from this belief in environmentalism—Easton's argument that African Americans were descended from the enlightened, peaceful civilizations of ancient Egypt and Africa, while white Americans were products of a European history filled with ignorance and violence. From the days of Noah and his children, Easton emphasized, as people had first migrated to differing climates and locales, "races" had emerged as the products of historically determined circumstances—that is, from differing cultural environments—not from differences in biology. Descendants of Noah who had wandered to harsh European climates had degenerated into savagery, Easton explained. Those who had the good fortune to settle in fertile Africa had created peaceful, learned, and wealthy civilizations, aspects of which were later adapted by southern Europeans through interaction with northern Africans, primarily Egyptians. "Races" that had evolved from such widely differing cultures confronted one another on a broader scale starting in the sixteenth century, Easton continued, when brutish Europeans invaded the rest of the world, obliterating America's Indians and turning millions of Africans into rootless aliens by destroying their cultures, kidnapping and enslaving them, and transporting them to the New World. Once Europeans had completed their terrible work, they had reduced once-glorious Africa to barbaric ignorance. Meanwhile, the United States grew ever more rich and powerful, feeding off the labor so cruelly extorted from generations of slaves.

Modern readers may sense in some of Easton's contentions strong overtones of "Afrocentrism," the controversial claims made by some contemporary writers that imperialistic, "white," Western civilization was built on cultural foundations "stolen" from "black" Africa or that black Americans, as descendants of the "humane" Africa of antiquity, are culturally superior to whites from "exploitative" Europe. Such similarities suggest the unusually broad sweep of Easton's historical vision: his recognition as early as the 1820s and 1830s of Africa's imaginative appeal in the minds of some American blacks, and his ability to raise questions of continuing importance. But while his explanations regarding Africa's history were both pathbreaking and original in scope and depth, he built his analysis, once again, from information and ideas with which he and many others had been long familiar.[33]

Members of the African American elite whom Easton knew well had also begun developing idealized images of Africa as early as the 1820s, particularly as their doubts increased as to the feasibility of achieving equality within the United States. In the 1820s and 1830s, travelers' descriptions of African culture and geography were widely published for the first time in the United States, and the history of ancient Egypt became a popular literary subject. Publications that Easton read closely, the African American–edited *Freedom's Journal* as well as tracts and articles of the American Colonization Society, developed positive accounts of African history and culture which stressed environmental explanations of racial differences.[34] Thus the originality and value of the Introduction, as of the *Treatise* as a whole, lie not in Easton's use of facts, but instead in his passion and his ability to establish a definitive explanation of racial oppression: how it developed from relations between Africa and Europe, how it was sustained, and how people can put an end to it.

Chapter 1 of the *Treatise* demonstrates just how consistently Easton pursued his environmentalist logic, even to its most painful conclusions. Expanding on "the Intellectual Character of the Colored People of the United States," he connects his history of Africa's glories and tragedies to the fate of black Americans living in his own day. Now he develops the idea that a brutal environment of racial oppression constructed by whites throughout the United States had literally transformed the descendants of "once noble" people into physically deformed and mentally stunted creatures.

Easton clearly indicts race-based slavery as the sole cause of such degradation. While granting that the debasing effects of slavery varied in proportion to the amount of time an individual and his ancestors had spent in bondage, Easton nevertheless insists that all descendants of African American slaves bore some mark of dehumanization. In making this statement he was even willing to include people like himself, a proud and accomplished free black born into a family three generations removed from slavery. Easton expresses this conviction in what is perhaps the most poignant personal statement in the *Treatise:*

> I wonder that I am a man; for though of the third generation from slave parents, yet in body and mind nature has never been permitted to half finish her work. Let all judge who is in the fault, God, or slavery, or its sustainers.

Near the end of the *Treatise* Easton develops this idea still further, arguing that the experience of enslavement was so comprehensively degrading to one's intellect and moral consciousness that even the most humane masters, intent on eventual emancipation of their slaves and on educating them in preparation for freedom, were probably wasting their efforts.

This particular theme in Easton's *Treatise* has the potential to conflict with the values of some readers today, and such a divergence is compounded when readers encounter Easton's next assertion that the abuse of pregnant African American women by cruel whites accounted for the biological transmittal of mental inadequacy and physical deformity to succeeding generations of blacks. A useful way to understand Easton's logic in developing these controversial assertions involves examining closely what he thought the various types of "racial characteristics" actually were. Since Easton wrote the *Trea-*

tise to persuade skeptical whites, it is impossible, of course, to rely on the document itself for the full range of his private views on this subject. Nevertheless, a critical and systematic reading of the *Treatise* can provide some well-founded conclusions.

The method involves a comparative analysis of crucial passages within the *Treatise,* an exercise that readers should undertake for themselves, but that might proceed as follows: first, one might consider Easton's list of the viscious stereotypes whites employed to denigrate African Americans and portray them as "degraded" people. Next, these stereotypes should be compared to the negative characteristics of maternal "impressions" which had been inflicted on pregnant slave women by the barbarities of slavery and racial oppression and then passed on to their children. Finally, both sets of racial influences should be set against Easton's description of the process of African American "redemption" and "transformation" that concludes the *Treatise.*

It becomes apparent, first, that Easton regarded certain specific physical traits—distended facial muscles, narrow foreheads, prominent eyeballs, hesitant speech, and downcast countenances—as outward physical *symptoms* of the deeper emotional damage wrought by racial oppression, not as biological evidence of "innate inferiority." With the cessation of racial oppression, Easton maintains, all of these characteristics would rapidly vanish, according to a transformation that he describes in detail. Apart from these physical manifestations of emotional oppression, Easton classifies all other examples of alleged African American "inferiority" as brutal, stigmatizing, white *interpretations* of perfectly normal African appearance. A flat nose, nappy hair, thick lips, dark color, and so forth were, in Easton's view, simply general characteristics of people of African ancestry and bore no relation whatsoever to inherent moral standing, intellectual capacities, or even any effects of slavery. In ancient Africa, after all, people possessing exactly these characteristics had, according to Easton, created magnificent civilizations which anyone would admire. In short, as Easton saw it, whites had combined the normal physiological traits of African people with the bodily manifestations of psychological and physical oppression to build bigoted fantasies and debasing stereotypes. They then invoked their own stereotypes to justify the continued exploitation of African Americans. Easton's vivid analysis of the mechanisms of segregation and oppression fills several angry pages of the *Treatise.*

In Easton's view, then, the debasement caused by white stereotyping and the actual physical damage caused by racial oppression had become intimately connected in a self-reinforcing cycle. But no matter how self-perpetuating he believed such oppression to be, Easton was always an environmentalist, insisting that the physical symptoms of race-based oppression were distributed among African Americans only according to the amount and duration of their exposure to it. In one part of the *Treatise,* for example, he makes plain his belief that symptoms of mental and physical disability could become fully developed only among "such as have become subject to slavery some considerable length of time." In other passages he insists that African immigrants fortunate enough to have avoided enslavement exhibited no such debilitating symptoms, and that African Americans from families long since emancipated were visibly recovering from traumas that had been endured by their forebears. In Easton's final vision of African American "redemption," he imagines the "transformation" and disappearance of furrowed brows, distended eyeballs, knotted muscles, and other symptoms of psychological distress and physical oppression. In a world governed by justice rather than by racial division, Easton promises, people who "looked like Africans" would take pride in their hair, noses, lips and color, appreciating their origins and regarding their appearance with healthy self-approval.

Contemporary readers are bound to have mixed reactions to Easton's writing. While his analysis of the brutalizing effects of racial oppression is powerful even today, some of his ideas—such as the notion that a pregnant woman can pass on acquired characteristics to her infant—seem absurd in the light of current knowledge. But however one might understand these discussions of black victimization, one sees that Easton possessed a remarkable ability to wrestle with complex issues of "race" which bedevil Americans still. And one, must, moreover, place his ideas in their larger historical context—the general current of thought from which Easton necessarily drew his own conclusions, as well as the particular audience to which his writing was addressed.

Easton's belief in the formative power of prenatal influence was widely shared by abolitionists and other reformers of the sort Easton knew well. Moreover, such concerns about the health of an expectant mother and its effect on her unborn child reflected these activists' religious convictions that the weakest and most helpless victims needed protection (not unlike the feelings of those who currently oppose abortion), and also their strong, instinctive feelings of revulsion against those who practiced physical cruelty. It was, in fact, emotions much like these that compelled visionaries like William Lloyd Garrison to take up the cause of abolition. Viewed in this context, Easton's vivid portrayal of African Americans as helpless victims was a product of the culture of his time and clearly designed to resonate with the values of his readers.[35]

Closely connected to these considerations of audience is the matter of Easton's rhetorical strategy. One must assume, after all, that he knew from his own experience what many talented historians would eventually teach us: that the day-to-day lives of countless African Americans disproved any claims of degradation and powerlessness. He had been closely associated for years with numerous free blacks, all powerful activists and some highly accomplished former slaves who were living denials of his assertions. He had met with them regularly in the National Colored Conventions and at ministerial conferences. More important, he had been welcomed into this distinguished circle of leaders because of his proud heritage as an accomplished member of the Easton family. His own family history was, in short, a fundamental contradiction to his portrayals of African Americans as helpless victims.

Further still, Easton knew well at least one free descendant of slaves who had attempted to overthrow the institution of slavery, Henry Drayton, an A.M.E. minister who had fled North after participating in the Denmark Vesey Conspiracy of 1822. Easton lived, moreover, in the aftermath of the Nat Turner insurrection, and undoubtedly he was well versed in the histories of Gabriel Prosser's insurrection and of the Haitian revolution, each a pivotal moment in the history of slave revolts. Nevertheless, at one point in the *Treatise* Easton states flatly that "a slave is metamorphosed into a machine," and that, once freed, "he is left a mere out-of-use wreck of machinery." He also cites the "indolent and degraded" former slaves of New York as evidence of a "degradation" so comprehensive that free blacks simply could not overcome it.[36]

Why did Easton override all this contrary knowledge when painting his bleak picture of African American powerlessness? The best answers are found in the ideological convictions of the specific audience to which Easton was writing. As noted earlier, he had come to regard himself at this point in his life as an apostle to the self-brutalizing and callous whites, leading them to redemption by showing them the magnitude of their crimes. However apathetic, uninformed, bigoted, and self-righteous American whites might be—and no matter how quick they were to blame the *victims* of white oppression—whites made up Easton's primary audience, and he could not afford to distract them with exceptions and counterexamples tangential to his fundamental point. It was *they* who had invented the agony of race, he insisted, and it was their responsibility to end it—not simply through apology, but most crucially by taking unprecedented *affirmative* steps to compensate those they had so grievously harmed. With the collapse of "uplift's " egalitarian promise, as Easton viewed it, no amount of African American initiative would suffice to bring forth the social transformation he now demanded.

Finally, as with the case of Easton's seemingly "Afrocentric" thinking, many of his claims of black people's powerlessness and degradation resonate powerfully with current ideological conflicts. From the 1960s and 1970s up to the present, civil rights activists, academicians, and public policy specialists continue to argue bitterly over claims, not unlike Easton's, that African Americans have been so heavily victimized by centuries of oppression that theirs has become a culture pathologically debilitated by the traumas of poverty, broken families, crime, isolation, and illiteracy.[37] Such contentions, of course, continue to echo loudly in ongoing (and heavily racialized) discussions of welfare programs, illegal drugs, teen-age pregnancy, and juvenile crime. Similarly, Easton's concern for the health of the unborn can be heard in discussions of racial issues that include pressing problems such as fetal alcohol syndrome, maternal drug addiction, lead poisoning, sexually transmitted diseases, and malnutrition. Judged from such contemporary perspectives, Easton's ideas of racial victimization continue to retain a disturbing pertinence as our society turns toward a new millennium.

Easton's solution for ending America's racial troubles—the notion with which he concludes the *Treatise,* that responsibility rests entirely with white Americans—also strikes a note of timelessness. It was whites, he emphasizes, who had uprooted unwilling Africans from their native lands. It was they, moreover, who had led a Revolution based on ideals of equality, only to violate these ideals by continuing to enslave and oppress fellow human beings. Now their only truly moral choice was to recognize blacks as fully credentialed American citizens. For as Easton emphasized when addressing the relationship of "race" to citizenship, "The claims the colored people set up . . . are the claims of an American. . . . Every child born in America, even if it be as black as jet, is American by birth and blood."

As God's creations and agents of his will, Easton emphasized, white Americans must reclaim their revolutionary promises. They must purge their souls of racial hatred, abolish slavery, sweep away prejudice, and initiate a program of spiritual, social, and economic reconstruction to return black Americans to their full humanity. For all his belief in the powerlessness of African Americans, Easton's providential faith remained at least as strong as it had been in his

1828 "Address." Now, however, it was white people, not African Americans, who needed God's intervention to fire their will for self-transformation. If whites truly did embrace God's designs, Easton prophesied, the African Americans' wounds would surely heal, blacks and whites would be joined in equality, and they would be reconciled with their Maker as well.

Although Easton's final demand in the Treatise for self-transformation aligned him with the Garrisonian abolitionists' call for a "moral revolution" within the souls of the white majority, evidence suggests, that by the time he was writing his *Treatise* he actually had grown impatient with white abolitionists. In one of their meetings he chided them for failing to recognize that "the spirit of slavery will survive in the form of prejudice, after the system is overturned." "Our warfare," he emphasized, "ought not to be against slavery alone, but against that spirit that makes color the mark of degradation." He could not have been reassured by Henry B. Stanton's reply that the American Anti-Slavery Society was already working to "kill both, if possible, with one blow."[38] For as his *Treatise* makes clear, Easton understood the power of bigotry as white leaders such as Stanton simply could not. To such moralists, white prejudice against African Americans was a sin, to be answered with scriptural denunciation. But as chapter 3 of the *Treatise* confirms in excruciating detail, it was to Easton a socially constructed force of enormous power, based ultimately on motives of basest greed, dominating the entire nation— the "free" North no less than the "slave" South—and invulnerable to preachments alone.

By 1837 most free African Americans had doubtless drawn these same conclusions. Sharing their hopelessness, anger, and frustration, Easton in his *Treatise* again embraced the redemptive Christianity of the 1828 "Address," but this time his demand was for fundamental change in the *behavior* of white people, not just for a softening of their hearts in response to African Americans' efforts at "uplift." The parable of the "Good Samaritan" provided the model. As the *Treatise* emphasizes in chapter 4, Jesus's illustration of spiritual and material charity is the teaching that, in the end, gave Easton the faith to believe that equality still numbered among God's promises.

Among those who had encountered the stranger attacked by thieves, Easton insisted, only the "Good Samaritan" responded as God had enjoined, by sharing not just his Christian sympathy but all of his worldly goods as well. The Samaritan alone had refrained from stepping to the opposite side of the road as the other passers-by had done. In Easton's final estimate, true emancipation would require, in similar fashion, morally transfigured whites who would also act like "Good Samaritans" by making full restitution to African Americans for all accumulated deprivations—both the material wealth the whites had stolen no less than the spiritual damage they had inflicted. As Easton expressed this idea, "Every collateral means would be marshalled under the heaven-born principle" of the Golden Rule:

> the emancipated must be placed back where slavery found them, and restore[d] to them all that slavery has taken away from them. . . . That only will open [the] . . . door . . . by which a reciprocity of sentiment and interest can take place—a proper knowledge acquired by the benefactor relative to his duty, and reciprocated on the part of the benefitted.

Then would God's creatures, black and white, finally be reconciled. African Americans would soon lose their symptoms of debasement and regain their underlying humanity, and they and their former oppressors would embrace one another in God's common family: "Their narrow foreheads, contracted for want of mental exercise, would begin to broaden. . . . That interior region, the dwelling place of the soul would be lighted up with the fire of love and gratitude. . . ." Easton put it most clearly in the *Treatise*'s final sentence: "And thus their whole man would be redeemed, rendering them fit for the associates of their fellow men in this life, and for the associates of angels in the world to come."

Thus Easton's final response to the troubles of a racialized nation, showed him to be a Christian environmentalist to the end, expressing views that, like so many of his other ideas, raised serious questions which have troubled us ever since. By calling for whites to restore to the "emancipated . . . all that slavery had taken away from them," Easton was clearly arguing from the principle of compensatory justice, contending that racial equality could not be achieved unless the disadvantages caused by past inequities were lessened for people of color. With this doctrine, Easton clearly anticipated the arguments of those later abolitionists and radical Republican legislators who would insist at the end of the Civil War that in order to insure equal opportunity in the defeated South, every family of emancipated slaves be granted at no cost "forty acres and a mule."[39] Much more recently, of course, the same philosophy has fired far-reaching controversy over the equitability of affirmative action programs and racial quotas or targets, the justice of racially based legislative redistricting, and the validity of demands by some African Americans for financial "reparations" to balance the accounts of slavery.

In 1859, on the eve of the Civil War, Easton's close friend and fellow Congregational minister, Amos G. Beman, predicted that "Long will the name of Rev. Hosea Easton, whose powerful mind knew no superior among the colored people of the country, be remembered." Roughly a decade later, Beman commented further on Easton, recalling that "We have had the instructions of some of the best minds of our race which the country has produced. Dr. Hosea Easton, a giant in his day, as many remember, lectured and wrote much."[40]

As it turned out, Beman's observations were more wish than fact. As the weight of evidence shows, Easton's example and ideas were seldom referred to by the powerful black abolitionists who followed him in the post-1840 era. For all their resonance with our contemporary racial preoccupations, Easton's views seem to have generated no following and little discussion as the ideology of black abolitionism continued to evolve before the Civil War. The failure of black chroniclers in the 1850s such as William Wells Brown and Martin Delany

Hosea and Louisa Easton's unmarked gravesites in Hartford's Old North Cemetery, with Hartford's present-day, predominantly African American, ghetto visible in the background. The cemetery, located at the intersection of Mather and Main Streets, was Hartford's designated burial place for Irish, Italian, Greek, Jewish, and "colored" families.

even to mention Easton's name, as well as its absence in the later works of Carter G. Woodson and Benjamin Quarles, also confirms Easton's historical obscurity. From the 1850s onward, only Beman, the Bostonian William Nell, and family members such as Benjamin Roberts and William Edgar Easton attempted to keep memories of James and Hosea Easton alive.[41]

Several factors explain this result. First and most simply, Easton died so soon after he published his *Treatise* that he had no opportunity to extend or defend his doctrines. More important, Easton's assertions that slaves and, perhaps more significantly, *former* slaves, had no capacity to resist whites and improve themselves did not sit well with such preeminent African American leaders as Frederick Douglass, William Wells Brown, Harriet Tubman, Martin Delany, and Sojourner Truth. Each, of course, was a prominent escapee from slavery whose life gave eloquent testimony to the substance of black resistance. Leading white abolitionists, in turn, promoted such impressive figures as spokespersons who could testify from direct personal experience about both the horrors of slavery and to the humanity and courage of the slaves. Judged against these ideological positions, much of Easton's thinking ran counter to the tactics and values of the abolitionist movement as it continued its struggles from the 1840s onward.[42]

But it must be emphasized once again that Easton designed his solutions to meet the circumstances of his time, not ours, and not Frederick Douglas's either. And certain crucial aspects of his thinking did prove to be of enduring value to the generation of black activists who took up his cause. Following the failure of self-initiated black "uplift," for example, Easton's contention that African Americans deserved compensatory justice held considerable appeal before the Civil War and took on paramount importance during Reconstruction once emancipation had actually been achieved. In addition, no pre–Civil War writer refuted the scientific claims of innate African inferiority more forcefully or intelligently than Easton did, or developed a more challenging explanation of racial differences and their implications. No one succeeded more convincingly in presenting racial oppression as a powerfully constructed human invention which, to be remedied, required material equality as well as moral revolution. And finally, by insisting that it was ultimately up to whites to end the agony of racial oppression, he paved the way for future generations of black leaders, who all would place a greater share of responsibility on those who maintained the evils of white supremacy and who most fully possessed the power to eliminate them.

As a result, Hosea Easton led his generation to see beyond the white-inflicted terrors of the 1830s, inviting those who came after him to set aside the impossible burden of an exclusively black movement of self-liberation. Never again, either before or after the Civil War, would African Americans preach to one another of "uplift" without also demanding that white oppressors give way.[43] No matter how poorly re-

membered Easton has been by those who continued his struggle, he
bestowed on them a legacy in which they all could take pride.

NOTES

1. The question of the Easton family's "mixed" lineage is important to explore in
detail, since it helps explain the sources of Hosea Easton's emphatic views that
"races" were not the result of biology, that all people are united by "one blood"
regardless of skin color, and that all descendants of Africans living in the United
States had become irreversibly "American." In *A Treatise on the Intellectual Character, and the Civil and Political Condition of the Colored People of the U. States; and
the Prejudice Exercised Towards Them: With a Sermon on the Duty of the Church to
Them* (Boston, 1837, and reprinted herein, 63–123), Hosea Easton characterizes
himself as being "of the third generation [removed] from slave parents." This means
that his great-grandparents were probably freed some time in the late seventeenth
or early eighteenth century, possibly by Peter Easton of Newport, Rhode Island,
or by his son, Nicholas. See John Osborne Austin, *The Genealogical Dictionary of
Rhode Island, Comprising Three Generations of Settlers Who Came before 1690*
(reprint, Baltimore, 1978), 293–95; and the will of Peter Easton, 26 April 1691, Collections of the Rhode Island Historical Society, Providence, Rhode Island. Though
Bradford Kingman, *A History of North Bridgewater, Massachusetts* (North Bridgewater, 1866), 209–10, William C. Nell, *Colored Patriots of the American Revolution*
(1855; reprint, Boston, 1969), 32–33, and Benjamin F. Roberts, "Our Progress in the
Old Bay State," *The New Era,* 31 March 1870, confirm James Easton's birth in
Middleborough, the town's records make no mention of him, leading one to surmise
that he probably lived beyond the town's outskirts where three Indian villages were
located, since free Indians were forbidden by law from living within the town. See
Middleborough's *Town Records Part I, 1658–1705.* Sarah Dunbar Easton, James's
wife, added to the family's multiracial character and its traditions of leadership. Her
father, Sampson Dunbar, is described in the town records of Braintree, Hingham,
and Stoughton as a "mulatto" of some substance who had business dealings with
Josiah Quincy Sr. Dunbar's second wife (Sarah's stepmother) "kept a school for
small children." See Waldo C. Sprague, *Genealogies of the Families of Braintree,
Massachusetts, 1640–1850* (Boston, 1912). The fact that Hosea Easton's uncle,
Samuel Dunbar, and Hosea's brother Caleb both married white women and that the
latter's wife, Chloe Packard, came from one of the leading families in North Bridgewater adds still further to the complex circumstances that informed Hosea's belief
in "one blood." For an excellent general treatment of the theme of multiracial-
ity in early New England, see Jack D. Forbes, *Africans and Native Americans*
(Champaign-Urbana, 1993), 190–271. For documentation on James Easton during
the Revolution and in North Bridgewater, see Kingman, *History of North Bridgewater,* 215, 317–19, 379, 497–98; Truxton Moebs, *Black Soldiers, Black Sailors,
Black Ink: Research Guide on African Americans in United States Military History,
1526–1980* (Chesapeake Bay and Paris, 1995), 423; Brockton, Massachusetts, *Vital*

Records (1850), 46, 197; Nell, *Colored Patriots,* 33–34; Plymouth, Massachusetts, Registry of Deeds, MF cards 1114, 4193, 7718, 8707. Our thanks go to David Ingram of Foxborough, Massachusetts, who supplied us with these records of real estate transactions which document the Easton family's land acquisitions in North Bridgewater from 1810 to the 1830s. For information about James Easton's arrival in North Bridgewater, the arrival of Sarah Dunbar, and their marriage, see Trustees and Memorial Committee of First Parish Congregational Church of Brockton, *A Coppying Out of ye Olde Recordes, Beginning With ye 4th Chh of Christ in Bridgewater—1740* (Brockton, Mass., 1980), 103, 105, 140–41, 194. Also, the *First Census of the United States of America, 1790, enumeration of the inhabitants of the town of Bridgewater, Massachusetts.*

2. Nell, *Colored Patriots,* 33–34; Kingman, *History of North Bridgewater,* 379. William Nell, a prominent Boston black abolitionist and sometime office manager for Garrison's *Liberator,* was clearly well acquainted with James Easton and his children. His reliability seems unquestionable since his information is confirmed in other primary sources, such as Roberts, "Progress" and Kingman, *History of North Bridgewater,* 209–10. On Nell's career, see Robert P. Smith, "William Cooper Nell: Crusading Black Abolitionist," *Journal of Negro History* 55 (July 1970): 182–99; and Dorothy Porter Wesley, "Integration versus Separation: William Cooper Nell's Role in the Struggle for Equality," in *Courage and Conscience: Black and White Abolitionism in Boston,* ed. Donald Jacobs (Bloomington, 1993). 207–24.

3. Nell, *Colored Patriots,* 33–34.

4. Roberts, "Progress"; The *Liberator,* 7 June 1834, 7 February 1835; Alice H. Easton to Samuel May Jr., 17 August 1851, Antislavery Collection, Boston Public Library; Moebs, *Black Soldiers,* 423. On the life and career of William Edgar Easton see Dickson D. Bruce, *African American Writing from the Nadir: the Evolution of a Literary Tradition, 1877–1915* (Baton Rouge, 1989), 11, 28–29, 39–40.

5. Studies of contemporaries of James Easton who embodied these values include Carol V. S. George, *Segregated Sabbaths: Richard Allen and the Rise of Independent Black Churches, 1760–1840* (New York, 1973); Shane White, *Somewhat More Independent: The End of Slavery in New York City, 1770–1810* (Athens, Ga., 1991); John Salliant, "John Teasman: African American Educator and the Emergence of Community in Early Black New York," *Journal of the Early Republic* 12 (fall 1992): 331–56; Ann Thomason, "James Forten and the Dream of the Raceless Republic" (undergraduate honors thesis, Macalester College, 1995).

6. The best general studies of the formation of free African American communities in the postrevolutionary North include James Oliver Horton and Lois E. Horton, *In Hope of Liberty: Culture, Community and Protest Among Northern Free Blacks* (New York, 1996); Gary B. Nash, *Forging Freedom: The Formation of Philadelphia's Black Community, 1720–1840* (Cambridge, Mass., 1988); Gary B. Nash and Jean Soderlund, *Freedom by Degrees: Emancipation in Pennsylvania and Its Aftermath* (New York, 1991); White, *Somewhat More Independent.* Joanne Pope Melish, *Disowning Slavery: Gradual Emancipation and the Cultural Construction of "Race" in New England, 1780–1860* (Ithaca, N.Y., 1998), offers a deep analysis of evolving and conflicting meanings of "race" in the North for free African Americans and for whites as well.

7. See Jack Weatherford, *Indian Givers: How the Indians of the Americas Trans-*

formed the World (New York, 1988); Jack Weatherford, *Native Roots: How the Indians Enriched America* (New York, 1991); Hermina Poatgieter, *Indian Legacy: Native American Influences on World Life and Culture* (New York, 1981); Joseph B. Oxendine, *American Indian Sports Heritage* (Champaign, Ill., 1988).

8. Paul Goodman's excellent article, "The Manual Labor Movement and the Origins of Abolitionism," *Journal of the Early Republic* 13 (fall 1993), charts the close relationship between white abolitionism and manual labor education as first practiced in Switzerland and Germany in the 1820s and then adopted in the United States. It does not recognize, however, that James Easton's venture preceded these developments by more than fifteen years. Other scholarship about the connection between abolitionism and labor education includes Charles A. Bennett's thorough research of industrial education, *History of Manual and Industrial Education Up to 1870* (Peoria, Ill., 1926); Virginia Dumas, "Hampton, Tuskeegee and Carlisle: Three Industrial Boarding Schools and Their Founding Zealots" (graduate paper, Northern Montana College, 1996; M. L. Barlow, *A History of Industrial Education in the United States* (Peoria, Ill., 1967).

9. Roberts, "Progress." Information conflicts as to the exact duration of the school's existence. Roberts states that the school closed after "a few years." The *Treatise* can be read as suggesting that it continued for between ten and twenty years. Kingman makes no mention of the manual labor school in his *History of North Bridgewater,* but reports that the factory began in "about 1814" and "continued in business for six years and failed" after which James Easton's sons Caleb and Sylvanus continued it "for ten years longer" until they retired (*History of North Bridgewater,* 379). This would bring the story to about 1830, the year that James Easton died and the family began to move on to shoemaking. It should be noted, however, that Kingman's account was written in 1866 and his estimate of the date of an occurrence that happened over fifty years earlier could not be as reliable as Hosea's 1837 account of an event that represented a major chapter in his short life. In a passage in which he is describing both the foundry and the school, Easton states that "the enterprise was followed for about twenty years," so it is not clear if he meant one, or the other, or both. If James Easton was one of the directors of the enterprise whose "hearts fell . . . in despair . . . and their bodies into their graves" because of their frustration and ultimately their failure in prevailing against the tide of prejudice, it would be safe to say that the business and school dissolved before his death in 1830. Also, since Hosea Easton makes no mention of, or allusion to, the business or its failure in the 1828 "Address," and since Hosea was still a resident of North Bridgewater in 1828, we may conclude that the Easton enterprise dissolved between 1828 and 1830.

10. *Freedom's Journal,* 25 April 1828; Hosea Easton, *An Appeal to the Christian Public in Behalf of the Methodist Episcopal Church* (Boston, 1828); Hosea Easton, "An Address: Delivered Before the Coloured Population of Providence, Rhode Island, on Thanksgiving Day, Nov. 27, 1828 by Hosea Easton of North Bridgewater, Mass" (Boston, 1828). As far as we can determine, only one original copy of this rare document is available for public reference, at the Library of Congress, Washington, D.C., which is the basis for our text, herein. William Lloyd Garrison, however, quoted from it in *Thoughts on Colonization* (Boston, 1832), 17–20, which suggests that it did gain some wider notice after its publication.

11. The best discussions of the ideology of African American "uplift" and respectability are found in James Oliver Horton and Lois E. Horton, "The Affirmation of Manhood: Black Garrisonians in Boston," in Jacobs, *Courage and Conscience,* 127–53; Horton and Horton, *In Hope of Liberty;* and Patrick Rael, "African American Elites and the Language of Respectability in the Antebellum North" (paper presented at the annual meeting of the Organization of American Historians, 1997). See also Fredrick Cooper, "Elevating the Race: The Social Thought of Black Leaders, 1827–1850," *American Quarterly* 24 (December 1972): 604–25.

12. Among the many studies that document these various trends are Leonard L. Richards, *"Gentlemen of Property and Standing": Antiabolitionist Mobs in Jacksonian America* (New York, 1970); Paul S. Gilje, *The Road to Mobocracy: Popular Disorder in New York City, 1763–1834* (Chapel Hill, 1987); George Frederickson, *The Black Image in the White Mind: The Debate on Afro-American Character and Destiny, 1817–1914* (New York, 1971), 3–27; Eric Lott, *Love and Theft: Blackfaced Minstrelsy and the American Working Class* (New York, 1993); David Roediger, *The Wages of Whiteness: Race and the Making of the American Working Class* (New York, 1991); Noel Ignatiev, *How the Irish Became White* (New York, 1995); Reginald Horsman, *Race and Manifest Destiny: The Origins of Racial Anglo-Saxonism* (Cambridge, Mass., 1981); Michael Kaplan, "New York City Tavern Violence and the Creation of a Male Working Class Identity," *Journal of the Early Republic* 15 (spring 1995):592–617.

13. See Shane White, " 'It Was A Proud Day': African Americans, Festivals and Parades in the North, 1741–1834," *Journal of American History* 81 (June 1994):13–50; and Nash, *Forging Freedom,* 67–211.

14. The most comprehensive survey of these developments remains Leon Litwack, *North of Slavery: The Negro in the Free States, 1790–1860* (New York, 1961). See also Emma Jones Lapsansky, " 'Since They Got Those Separate Churches': Afro-Americans and Racism in Jacksonian America," *American Quarterly* (spring 1980):122–39; Emma Jones Lapsansky, *Neighborhoods in Transition: William Penn's Dream and Urban Reality* (New York, 1994), 71–151; William H. Pease and Jane H. Pease, *Black Utopias: Negro Communal Experiments in America* (Madison, Wisc., 1963); Richard H. Wade, "The Negro in Cincinnati, 1800–1830," *Journal of Negro History* 39 (January 1954): 49–51; John M. Werner; "Race Riots in the United States in the Age of Jackson, 1824–1849" (Ph.D. diss., University of Indiana, 1973). On the specific relationship of the history of Indian removal to abolitionism and the themes of racial "uplift," see Brian W. Dippe, *The Vanishing American: White Attitudes and United States Indian Policy* (Middletown, Conn., 1982), 89–103; Linda Kerber, "The Abolitionist Perception of the Indian," *Journal of American History* 62 (September 1975):271–95. Andrew Jackson evicted the Cherokees and many other eastern tribes from their homelands to a forced exile in "Indian Territory" (now Oklahoma) in open defiance of a Supreme Court decision of 1831 (Worcester v. Georgia), in which the court ruled that the Indian Removal Act of 1830 was unconstitutional.

15. See P. J. Stadenraus, *The African Colonization Movement, 1816–1865* (New York, 1961), 94–187; Frederickson, *Black Image,* 1–127; Alison Freehling, *The Drift toward Dissolution: The Virginia Slavery Debate of 1831–32* (Baton Rouge, 1982); David Brion Davis, "Reconsidering the Colonization Movement: Leonard Bacon and

the Problem of Evil," *Intellectual History Newsletter* 14 (1992):3–16; Hugh Davis, "Northern Colonization and Free Blacks, 1823–1827: A Case Study of Leonard Bacon," *Journal of the Early Republic* 17 (winter 1997):651–675.

16. David Walker, *Appeal . . . to the Coloured Citizens of the World,* ed. Charles Wiltse (1829; reprint, New York, 1965), 67–68. For an extremely revealing treatment of David Walker, see Peter Hinks, *To Awaken my Afflicted Brethren: David Walker and the Problem of Antebellum Slave Resistance* (College Station, Pa., 1997).

17. See Bruce Dain, "A Hideous Monster of the Mind: American Race Theory, 1787–1859" (Ph.D. diss., Princeton University, 1996), 96–157; and Bruce Dain, "Haiti and Egypt in Early Black Racial Discourse in the United States," *Slavery and Abolition* 13 (December 1993):139–61. For a very stimulating reconsideration of black and white abolitionist activities and strategies from the 1790s onward, which led to the Convention movement and black-white collaborations in the early 1830s, see Richard Newman, "The Transformation of American Abolition: People, Tactics and the Changing Nature of Activism, 1780s–1830s" (Ph.D. diss., State University of New York, Buffalo, 1997).

18. For information about the Convention movement, see Julie Winch, *Philadelphia's Black Elite: Activism, Accommodation and the Struggle for Autonomy* (Philadelphia, 1988); Howard Holman Bell, *A Survey of the Negro Convention Movement, 1830–1861,* (New York, 1953; reprint, New York, 1969); Howard Holman Bell, ed., *Minutes of the Proceedings of the National Negro Conventions, 1830–1864* (New York, 1969).

19. See Bell, *Minutes* [1831], 6; [1832], 4, 8, 32–35; [1833], 7–10, 18. On the ongoing convention discussion of the Jocelyn, Tappan, Garrison manual labor proposal see Bell, *Survey,* 20–26. For wider perspectives on this initiative, see James Brewer Stewart, *William Lloyd Garrison and the Challenge of Emancipation* (Arlington Heights, Ill., 1992), 59–61; Bertram Wyatt-Brown, *Lewis Tappan and the Evangelical War against Slavery* (Cleveland, 1969), 87–91. Several letters exchanged between Garrison and Jocelyn on this subject are in the collections of the Connecticut Historical Society.

20. For a modern, interpretative overview of the abolitionist movement after 1831, the rise of the doctrine of "immediate emancipation," and the white abolitionists' rejection of colonization, consult James Brewer Stewart, *Holy Warriors: The Abolitionists and American Slavery* (New York, 1997).

21. The fullest account of these developments is found in Leonard P. Curry, *The Free Black in Urban America, 1800–1850* (Chicago, 1981), 196–215.

22. For details of the suppression of the New Haven manual labor college, see Robert Austin Warner, *New Haven Negroes: A Social History* (New Haven, 1940), 50–55.

23. See Richards, *"Gentlemen of Property,* 20–155.

24. On Garrison's English fund-raising failures, see Stewart, *Garrison,* 63–68, and John L. Thomas, *The Liberator: William Lloyd Garrison, A Biography* (Boston, 1965), 156–66. For accounts of the divisions within white abolitionism, see Aileen Kraditor, *Means and Ends in American Abolitionism: Garrison and His Critics on Strategy and Tactics* (New York, 1969); and James Brewer Stewart, "Peaceful Hopes and Violent Experiences: The Evolution of Radical and Reforming Abolitionism, 1831–1837," *Civil War History* 17 (December 1971):293–309.

25. The *Emancipator,* 17 February 1835. The announcement of the founding of the institution appeared in the *Emancipator,* 1 April 1834. For an account of the riot, see John W. Stedman, *Scrapbooks on Hartford, Connecticut History, 1784–1894,* 4 vols., collections of the Connecticut Historical Society.

26. Edward Abdy, *Journal of a Residence and Tour in the United States of North America, April, 1833–October, 1834* (London, 1835), 3:206–207. For an account of the riots, see the Hartford *Courant,* 15 June 1835.

27. This event can be surmised from the final page of Easton, *Treatise,* which states that the proceeds from the sale of the pamphlet were to be dedicated "to a colored society in Hartford Con., who have lost their meeting-house by fire." The "society" referred to may have been the Hartford Literary and Religious Institution mentioned above, but even if that were the case, it is likely that the society would have been meeting in Easton's A.M.E. Church in the first place, rather than ex- pending scarce funds on its own building. Black churches in other northern cities served as headquarters for many self-help and activist groups, and therefore it was probably Easton's church itself that burned. See Roy Finkenbine, "Boston's Black Churches: Institutional Centers of the Antislavery Movement," in Jacobs, *Courage and Conscience: Black and White Abolitionists in Boston,* 169–89; and Carol V. R. George, "Widening the Circle: Black Churches and the Abolitionist Crusade, 1830– 1860," in *Antislavery Reconsidered: New Perspectives on the Abolitionists,* ed. Lewis Perry and Michael Fellman (Baton Rouge, 1979), 75–95. A careful search of the Hartford *Courant* for 1836–37 yields no information on the fire, but an article from the Concord, New Hampshire, *Observer,* reprinted in the *Liberator,* 14 April 1837, reports that after Easton had finished speaking, he "took up a collection to aid in the rebuilding of an African church in Hartford, Con.," a comment which leaves little doubt that it was, in fact, Easton's church that had burned. The authors wish to thank Kathryn Viens, who through the good offices of Richard Newman, shared a copy of Jennie F. Copeland, "Mansfield in Other Days," the *Mansfield (Massachu- setts) News,* 27 March 1937, which reprints a report of Easton's appearance before a white audience "to speak on the needs of the free colored people and to solicit subscriptions to rebuild a church for the colored people of Hartford."

28. *Observer,* Concord, N.H., reprinted in the *Liberator,* 14 April 1837.

29. The *Liberator,* 13 March 1837, 3.

30. In early 1837, Easton registered some of his clearly skeptical views on the efficacy of slave insurrections in a resolution before the annual meeting of the Mas- sachusetts Anti-Slavery Society which argued that "the spirit of insurrection and insubordination of the slave population of this country is restrained more by the influence of the free colored population thereof than by all the oppressive legislative enactments of the slave holding States." See the *Liberator,* 11 February 1837.

31. Chapter 3 of the *Treatise* offers particularly compelling descriptions of his day-to-day encounters with prejudice. Dain, in "Hideous Monster," 164–94, pro- vides a valuable interpretation of Easton's *Treatise* as a systematic analysis of the problem of "race."

32. On environmentalism's relationship to abolitionism in general, see Freder- ickson, *Black Image,* 3–27; Robert H. Abzug, *Cosmos Crumbling: American Reform and the Religious Imagination* (New York, 1994); and Ronald Walters, *The Antislav- ery Appeal: American Abolitionism after 1830* (Baltimore, 1976), 37–70.

33. Dain, in "Hideous Monster," 188–92, provides a close evaluation of the pertinence of Easton's thinking to modern "Afrocentrism." In our reading of the *Treatise,* Easton's contrast between whites as products of a barbaric history and blacks as descendants of ancient Africa's glory has little to do with assertions of African American cultural superiority and much more to do with his sense of republican outrage at white society's betrayal of the egalitarian gains of the American Revolution. His strenuous assertions that African Americans had been irretrievably cut off from Africa, together with his emphatic defense of the American Revolution, seem to us to reveal Easton as much more a radical American republican than an African American cultural nationalist. For Easton's view of the Revolution, see chapter 2 of the *Treatise,* below. For discussions of modern "Afrocentric" thinking, consult Martin Bernal, *Black Athena: The Afro-Asiatic Roots of Classical Civilization: The Fabrication of Ancient Greece, 1787–1985* (London, 1987); Mary R. Lefkowitz, *Not Out of Africa: How Afrocentrism Became an Excuse to Teach Myth as History* (New York, 1996); Clarence Walker, *Deromanticizing Black History: Critical Essays and Reappraisals* (Knoxville, Tenn., 1991); Chancellor Williams, *The Destruction of Black Civilization: Great Issues of Race from 4500 B.C. to 200 A.D.* (Chicago, 1974); Cheikh Anta Diop, *Civilization or Barbarism: An Authentic Anthropology* (Chicago, 1988).

34. See Dain, "Haiti."

35. On these various points see Elizabeth B. Clark, " 'The Sacred Rights of the Weak': Pain, Sympathy and the Culture of Individual Rights in Antebellum America," *Journal of American History* 82 (September 1995):463–93.

36. For evidence of Easton's association with Drayton, see the *Liberator,* 10 June 1837, which contains Drayton's obituary, written by Easton.

37. For a sense of these controversies of the 1960s and 1970s consult Stanley Elkins, *Slavery: A Problem in American Institutional and Intellectual Life* (Chicago, 1959); Ann Lane, ed., *The Debate over Slavery: Stanley Elkins and His Critics* (Champaign-Urbana, 1971); and the famous report on the status of African American families developed under the direction of U.S. Senator Daniel Patrick Moynihan, published by the U.S. Department of Labor, *The Negro Family: The Case for National Action* (Washington, D.C., 1965).

38. The *Liberator,* 11 February 1837.

39. The fullest recent account of the struggle for racial equality after the Civil War is Eric Foner, *Reconstruction: America's Unfinished Revolution* (New York, 1991).

40. Amos G. Beman Scrapbooks, vol. 2, Beinecke Library, Yale University.

41. See Nell, *Colored Patriots,* 32–33; Roberts, "Progress"; William Wells Brown, *The Rising Son; or the Antecedents and Advancement of the Colored Race* (Boston, 1876); Martin R. Delany, *The Condition, Elevation, Emigration and Destiny of the Colored People of the United States* (New York, 1852); Carter G. Woodson, *Negro Orators and Their Orations* (1925; reprint, New York, 1969). Benjamin Quarles, *The Black Abolitionists* (New York, 1969), 72, mentions Easton's name, but nothing substantial about his life or career. As this volume went to press, however, a newly published book suggests that historical interest in Easton's life and writings is reviving. See Joanne Pope Melish, *Disowning Slavery: Gradual Emancipation and "Race" in New England, 1780–1860* (Ithaca, N.Y.: Cornell University Press, 1998) for a valuable analysis of gradual slave emancipation and evolving problems of

"race" in the free states which presents Easton as a particularly acute observer and thinker about the racial dynamics of his day.

42. On this point, see especially David Blight, *Frederick Douglass' Civil War: Keeping Faith in Jubilee* (Baton Rouge, 1989), 1–81.

43. This new formulation, linking "uplift" and equality with uncompromising demands on white society, is comprehensively set forth as a transition in black activism from "moral reform" to "independence" in Peter Ripley et al., eds., *Witnesses for Freedom: African American Voices on Race, Slavery and Emancipation* (Chapel Hill, 1993), 1–28 and in David Blight, *Frederick Douglass' Civil War,* 1–100. This point, however, was made most forcefully as part of the Easton family's ongoing tradition of activist leadership in the career of Benjamin F. Roberts, Hosea Easton's nephew (son of his sister, Sarah, and Robert Roberts). While acting as a driving force in Massachusetts school desegregation struggles in the early 1850s, Roberts also published a short-lived newspaper, tellingly named the *Self-Elevator.* See Robert L. Hall, "Massachusetts Abolitionists Document the Slave Experience," in Jacobs, *Courage and Conscience,* 85.

AN ADDRESS:

Delivered before the

COLOURED POPULATION,

of Providence, Rhode Island,

on Thanksgiving Day,

Nov. 27, 1828

It was not expected at the time, by the Author of this work, that he should be solicited for a copy for publication; but by the ardent request of a Committee chosen for that purpose, by the Coloured Population of Providence, he was influenced to yield to their solicitation. Under such circumstances, and the short space of time he had to prepare it for the Press, he hopes, should the wise and learned find anything in it, strenuously represented, they will make all due allowances; as the Author has experienced the heart-rending deprivations of Liberty, as described in the following pages-both in his private, as well as public course of life.

ADDRESS.

MEN AND BRETHEREN —This is a day set apart by our Rulers as a day of rejoicing for the many blessings enjoyed, while greater prospects of plenty and happiness are continually heaving in view. We, as a nation, have great reason to rejoice, that by the great wheel of Providence, prosperity has graced our train while marching up the hill of popularity & honour. Let the expanding mind reflect for a moment, the rapid growth of this Nation, from the time a little handful held their council upon Plymouth Beach, until the present time. And if their hearts are not under the influence of a sordid disposition, they will to day tune them in anthems of praise and thanksgiving to God, for thus rearing us from nothing, to a great and mighty nation.

I repeat again, that prosperity has graced our train. Prosperity has opened the door of the forest for the reception of our forefathers; granting them an opportunity to display their superior knowledge in the use of fire arms above that of the natives: by which means the latter were drove out before them, being slain by thousands, thus, leaving them in peaceable possession of the soil. Again, Prosperity did attend their endeavours to introduce agriculture, the mechanic arts, and scientific knowledge. Prosperity did also aid their labours while propagating religious principles through our Republic, insomuch, that there is not a city, town, or hardly a neighborhood, but in which you will find a temple of worship, said to be erected to the worship of God. In a word, whatever course we have taken, the wheel of providence has led us into a field of prosperity. The memorable fourth of July, brings into our view, that important era of our country, when her liberties were threatened by England's pride. But methinks, I hear, a brave Washington, standing on his dignified eminence, exclaiming! Liberty! Liberty! Liberty! Or death. His valiant confederates rejoin'd the theme, and ere long, every heart burned with the fire of Liberty. The Ensign of Liberty was hoisted, and manfully defended. A Constitution was wisely framed, declaring all men to be free and equal. Who can say that our constitution is not founded on the principles of liberty and equality! We are indebted, then to divine providence for thus prospering our march as a nation. Many other blessings that we enjoy, might be brought into notice. But time will not permit us even to contemplate one out of ten thousand of the blessings we enjoy daily. How animating then is the *celubrious* [salubrious] sound of Liberty. The voice of Liberty calls the energies of the human soul to emerge out of nature's darkness, and to explore divine spiritual principles; from thence to angelic. How admirable it is, that the higher the soul arises by being expanded by intelligent perception, the more it breathes forth praise and thanksgiving to God, still beholding momentarily new delights in the vast field of Liberty, which God has given it for an inheritance, it bursts forth in the inspired language of the Psalmist. "It is a good thing to give thanks unto the Lord, and to sing praises to thy name, O, most high. For thou Lord hast made me glad through thy work. I will triumph in the work of thy hands." Again—If we follow the same train of reflection in natural intelligence, we shall find that liberty has proportionably the same effect and proffers the same reward. In this, our country, how soon do we see the infant grow to a stature which qualifies him to fill the highest seat of honour among our rulers? And thus be able to rejoice to see the expanded wings of Liberty, brooding over her votaries, sheltering them from slavery and oppression. But while I have endeavored to inspire your hearts with thankfulness to God, there has reflections forced themselves into my mind which has caused me to tremble for the fate of this country. O, America! Listen to your subjects. Allied to you by birth and blood. Shut out from all slavery which you have rivetted on their necks. Look at Virginia! Look at Washington! See droves of your subjects coupled together by pairs, while others are administering the laws of Liberty. And to fill out the file, we see those, who have received the dignified appellation of "Negro Drivers," inflicting merciless stripes upon their fellow subjects; drawing forth that sacred blood which God has forbidden to be shed; forcing their march, some from wives, some from parents, some from children, others from all that is near and dear to them. And for what? To gratify the avarice of proud America. O, Liberty, where art thou! Is this all? No! We will pass on. Leaving behind thought the barbarous cruelty imposed upon the natives, & as to the hellish practice of importing a foreign nation to a country of liberty, to be sold in slavery; it were better to be buried in oblivion and remembered no more forever. There are about 500,000 of the above named degraded sufferers, who are said to be free, which assertion I deny. It is true, we live under a milder State Administration at present. It is also true, that we are in some respects exalted to heaven, in point of Liberty, above that of our fellow subjects, who are under the immediate scourge of avarice. Their awful situation, doubtless, many of you have experienced, who compose this respectable auditory—while others of you have been eye witnesses to the bloody scenes of cruelty and murder. Bretheren, what was the sensation of your minds, when you beheld many of the female sex, pregnant with their young, tied to a tree or stake, and whipt by their masters, until nature gave way, and both mother and infant yielded up the ghost, while bearing the hellish scourge of these candidates for hell? What were they, when you saw your bretheren shot or beat with clubs? When you saw their master vent his rage, by murdering them by degrees, either, by roasting them alive, dissecting them limb by limb, or starving them to death for not complying with their unjust requirements? What were they, when you beheld the youth massacred for the smallest misdemeanor, and their affectionate parents not daring to make the least resistance for fear of falling victims to the same fate? What were they, when you saw the disciples of Christ, denied the privilege of meeting in groves and by-lots, to worship their God as guided by his spirit? What were they, I would ask, when you saw these things and many more, in the very heart of our country—A country of Liberty—Near the very seat of Government? Did not the spirit of Liberty cry within you, for vengeance to fall upon this country, which has so falsified the principles of Liberty, and trampled justice under foot. Now as we compose a part of the number who are said to be free, of course it becomes our duty to consider how far our liberty extends. The first enquiry is, Are we eligible to an office? No.—Are we considered subjects of the government? No.—Are we initiated into free schools for mental improvement? No.—Are we patronised as salary men in any public business whatever? No.—Are we taken into social compact with Society at large? No.—Are we patronised in any branch of business which is sufficiently lucrative to raise us to any material state of honour and respectability among men, and this, qualify us to demand respect from the higher order of society? No.—But to the contrary. Everything is withheld from us that is calculated to promote the aggrandizement and popularity of that part of the community who are said to be the descendants of Africa. I am sensible the white population will deny the fact above stated. But to confirm the fact, let us notice our ordinary course since the American Independence.

We will notice, first, our march in religious improvement. God has raised up some able ambassadors of truth among our population; and though they are held in contempt among the whites, yet God has caused his light to shine through them, to the great shame of our oppressors; and has decided the question, respecting the natural intelligence of the sable race, which has so long employed the pen of learned interrogators. But where are their privileges? Where even they can embody a little handful of coloured people together, there they can display their respective talents, as long as the means of subsistence is left them, but when that is exhausted, they are compelled to appeal to day labour for support. Or should they obey the heavenly command to "go into all the world and preach the gospel to every creature," they would often be treated with contempt by those that ought to be their patrons. Should one enter a town or city, with his credentials, and offer them to the minister of the church, it is more than probable, that the best appointments the minister would make for him, to discharge his duty, would be at a private house on a week day. Should he stop over the Sabbath, he would be introduced into the most remote part of the house of God, that is too demeaning to have the beasts for its occupants. How does he fare on his journey from place to place? I am bold to say that he cannot purchase a seat in the public stage, only by sufferance. I have known men of that profession, to be detained in towns and cities, not far distant from this place, ten days, before they could prosecute their journey; and then be under the necessity of getting some white man as an intercessor to the driver or owners for a passage on the outside of the carriage, by paying full price for fare. I know of an occurrence which took place in a stage passing from New Bedford to Fall River. It appears that two coloured men paid their passage upon the above named rout, they being the only passengers, occupied the back seat. When they arrived at West-port village, there was a white sailor of low grade, and a young girl that worked in the Factory, that made application for a passage to Fall River. They were immediately gallanted to the stage, the door was thrown open, and orders given by the driver, for the colored men to take the forward seats, which were complied with; when the two genteels got into the carriage and took the highest seat. One of these coloured gentlemen, was a minister of the gospel, of no mean standing; and what must have been his feelings, God only knows.

We will now notice our means of acquiring literary information. It is true, that in our northern States, the laws have made provisions for us without distinction. But though we claim our right lawfully, yet, like all our other rights, we are denied enjoyment of them. We send our children to primary schools among white children; and if there is any demeaning place of contempt, to be found in any part of the School

Room, there is the place for our children to get their information; while the little flax-headed boys and girls, are learnt by their parents to place a reproach upon them, by calling them Negroes, and the place where they are destined to sit, negro seats. Thus, our poor youth are discouraged, disheartened, and grow up in ignorance; fitted only to be an object of ridicule and contempt through life, by the higher order of Society. Some, doubtless, will be ready to say, that our liberty is above this. In answer to whom I will acknowledge that there is an exception in States and Cities. In New York and Connecticut, the coloured population are brought more into public notice, as well as in the cities of New York and Boston; also, in many other places, public support for schools is set apart for the coloured population. In those schools, we have youths well qualified for the common business of life; but when they have obtained their education, they know enough only to feel sensible of their misery. Their minds being expanded, their perception brightened, their zeal ardent for promotion; they look around for business, they find that custom cuts them off from all advantages. They apply to merchants to patronise them as Clerks, they are rejected. They apply to attornies at law to receive them into their office, they are rejected. They apply to the mariner, they are rejected, except, to go before the mast, cook, or steward. They apply to Mechanics of different occupations, here, too, they are rejected. And for what? Because it is customary. Leaving law, justice, and equity altogether out if the question. And should it become customary to cut off a black man's head, (as it is already at the south,) then of course we must lose our head, if custom says it is right. We see then the situation of our youth, turned out of doors without the least encouragement whatever. Now let us notice the consequence. Those bright minds enlarged by education, being under the necessity of taking up some low calling, which is not calculated to satisfy the extention of them, they become like the starving man, who, for the want of wholesome food, partakes of that which is poisonous and destructive. So it is with our youth, for the want of those encouragements set up before them, that is calculated to draw their attention to the pursuits of honour, respectability, virtue and industry, their expanded minds relapse into sordid dissipation, and fall victim to all the vices and folly incident to discouraged minds; and thus, the more education they have, under such circumstances, the more artful they are in following the haunt of dissipated principles. O, shocking! Is America to answer for all this? When then does justice sleep? It is true, that many of our population survive the struggle, so far as to arise to a degree of respectability. But with what respect are they treated? Let the man of business travel through the northern states. And I am ready to prove to you, that he will not pass ten miles, without meeting with insults almost sufficient to enrage a saint. If he hires his passage in the stage, he must be posted up with the driver to suffer the severity of the weather. When the passengers stop to dine, he must take his fare in the cook room, with the cook. And for a sitting parlour, he must take the bar-room; to have his feelings injured by tavern haunters and drunkards. If you look for his lodging chamber, you will find it in the garret, or back clutter chamber. These are fine places for men of business. Under these, and other disadvantages, we see the man is not calculated to do business, for the want of society. Society is the very mother who supplies men of business with useful knowledge; for the want of which, the poor man lays out his money at 75 per cent, disadvantage; and to discourage and depress his mind still further, the question is asked by the whites: Why is it that Negroes cannot do business like other people? Again—Should any one become religious, and feel desirous to follow the precepts of his Lord and Master, by having his name enrolled in the Church Militant, he is there treated more like a beast than in any other course of life. How say you? I answer—The coloured "brother," however able to provide for himself, must have a place provided for him. And where is it? In some remote part of the Meeting-House, or in a box built above the gallery. When the Church is called to partake of the sacred elements, the black communicants must come down, stand or sit in some remote part of the lower floor, until the white bretheren have eat what they want of the Lord's body, and drank what they want of his blood; then cries the minister, "Come coloured bretheren, now come and partake of the broken body of Christ. It is free for all without any distinction." And it is a chance if he does not, while thus officiating, offer an insult to their feelings, by saluting them as Africans or Ethiopians. While in fact they are Americans, and perhaps distantly related to some of the white members, by reason of the brutal conduct of their fathers. Now these are facts. There is not a church in the circle of my knowledge but what, must bear the character above asserted. And can rational beings, believe that God is a fool, that he is well pleased with such idolatry? We will follow this subject a little further, and see if we cannot find other things that gives character to a Christian nation. It is an obvious fact, that the white population are alarmed at the rapid growth of the coloured people; insomuch, that there is not a soul, that has any forecast, but that is troubled; and I would to God, that they might be confounded in their own craft, until, brought to experience true repentance, and are willing to deal justly with their neighbors.

The *Colonizing Craft* is a diabolical pursuit, which a great part of our Christian community are engaged in. Now bretheren, I need not enlarge on this point. You that have been observing, have already seen the trap under the bait; and although some of our population, have been foolish enough to sell their birthright for a mess of pottage, yet I doubt, whether the Colonization Society will entrap many more. It is too barefaced, and contrary to all reason, to suppose, that there is any good design in this project. If they are willing to restore four-fold for what they have been taken by false accusation, they can do it to better advantage in the bosom of our country, than at several thousand miles off. How would you do, bretheren, if your object was really to benefit the poor? Would you send them into a neighboring forest, and there deal out that food which they were famishing for? Now we stand different from beggars. Our ancestors were stolen property, and property which belonged to God. This is well known by our religious community; and they find that the owner is about to detect them. Now if they can slip away these stolen goods, by smuggling all those out of the country, which God would be likely to make an instrument of, in bringing them to justice, and keeping the rest in ignorance; by such means, things would go on well with them, and they would appease their consciences by telling what great things they are doing for the coloured population and God's cause. But we understand better how it is. The deception is not so well practised, but that we can discover the mark of the beast. They will steal the sons of Africa, bring them to America, keep them and their posterity in bondage for centuries, letting them have what education they can pick up of themselves; then transport them back to Africa; by which means America gets all her drudgery done at little expense, and endeavor to flatter [the] Deity, by making him a sacrifice of good works of this kind. But to the awful disappointment of all such blasphemers, they will meet the justice of God, which will be to them a devouring sword.

TO CONCLUDE.

BRETHEREN—My heart is filled with sorrow for this nation. I am far from being envious, and I would caution you against any revengeful or malignant passions; but stand still and see the salvation of God. Stand still did I say? Yes, so far as it respects the providence of God; we are to stand still, look, wonder, and adore. But as it respects the great labour and ardent zeal which involves upon us at the present day; there is no time to stand still. The time has come, when our necessities calls aloud for our exertions, to prepare ourselves for the great events which are about heaving in view. Bretheren, the dreary night of darkness, which our fathers passed through, is about to disperse. And notwithstanding we are a divided people, tossed to and fro, and hunted like the partridge upon the mountain, yet the glorious rays of rational intelligence and literary acquirements, are beginning to backen the chaos darkness, which has so long pervaded the minds of our population. Yes, bretheren, let a theme of praise and thanksgiving to God, thrill through every heart, in silent accents; for the sunbeams of Liberty are casting forth their glorious rays through the eastern atmosphere; and we may rationally entertain the hope, that

God, in his wise Providence, will cause this glorious sun to arise to its meridian, and burst those fetters with which we are bound, and unlock the prison doors of prejudice; granting us Liberty to enjoy the blessings of life like other men. But we must not suppose that we shall obtain those blessings without our co-operation with divine order; for, inasmuch as mankind are created intelligent beings, and recipient forms, it follows, that every principle, whether natural or spiritual, is obtained by the rational principle which is always found with man; that turning itself toward divine order, they join hands as companions, co-operate with each other, and thus, they become the parents which begets understanding to recipient man. What I wish to be understood by divine order, are those principles or attributes of light, which, in the order of providence flow to man. Now all persons that have arrived to the years of discretion, have already a degree of understanding, which enables them to perceive the duty that is set before them. Then as it respects our community, it is plain to see, by the foregoing statements, respecting our oppresst community, what is necessary. It is evident that we ought to turn our attention to moral improvement. A principle of jealousy one towards another, has become almost hereditary; which prevents any combined operation among us. The first thing necessary, is, to cultivate the principles of concord and unanimity among ourselves, that we may become aids to each other; for the prosecution of which, we ought to introduce operations that is accordant with the object in pursuit. In all cases of improvement, there must be an object set up with way-marks, that are calculated to attract the mind from a low state to higher attainments. If then, we can combine our ability, and bend it this course, it will open a field of labour for the reception of our youth, who are coming upon the stage of action, and give them an opportunity of displaying their intellectual talents; which will give a character to our community, and take away our reproach. When our operations become united, that the voice of our community, may be heard as the voice of one man; then shall we be able to control the principles of indolence and immorality of every species, and inculcate those of industry and virtue, with all qualifications necessary to enable us to control the effects of our own labour, and make it subservient to the benefit of our own community. We may look abroad and see sufficient to induce us to become active in our own interest. You, that are the fathers of our community, ought to use your feeble efforts to the establishment of the temple of Liberty; and when your sun shall hide itself beyond the western region, it shall leave a principle enstampt upon rising generations, which will embellish our bright prospects, and entail honours to your name while time shall last. Mothers, you have something to do with this important undertaking. Your virtuous council to your daughters, will qualify them to become useful in their circles. By which means, the haunt of the dance-hall will be broken. Bretheren, the time has come, when you, that are in the meridian of life, ought to raise the voice of Liberty and equality: truth and justice: virtue and industry, both by example and precept. I would also encourage the female part of our community, in the language of the people of Israel to Boaz, "The Lord make the woman that is come into thy house, like Rachel and Leah; which two, did build the house of Israel; and do thou worthily in Ephratah, and be famous in Bethlehem. And let thy house, be like the house of Pharez, whom Tamar bare unto Judah, of the seed which the Lord shall give thee of this young woman." So let it be concerning you. The Lord make you to our community, like Rachel and Leah; which two, did build the house of Israel; and do thou worthily in Ephratah, and be famous in Bethlehem. And let thy house, be like the house of Pharez, whom Tamar bare unto Judah, of the seed which the Lord shall give thee of this young woman. But my dear youth what shall I say to you? Can I make use of any language that will detach your minds from delusive pleasures, and cause you to look to the great object of your interest. Remember, my young friends, that your fathers were deprived the opportunity you now enjoy; and while I am addressing you, methinks I hear a voice from the graves of our fathers! And what is the language? It calls on you to forsake those foolish practices, which are so common amongst us; and apply your hearts to wisdom.

{ 61 }

"An Address"

It is no time, my young friends, to spend your time in the dance-hall. It is no time to exercise your ability in gambling. But you must lay aside all unnecessary diversion, and alter your courses; Come out of this degrading course of life; Distinguish yourselves as pious, industrious, and intelligent men and women. This will demand respect from those who exalt themselves above you. I must now leave this subject with you, hoping that this day's labour will not be in vain; for I assure you my heart mourns daily, while beholding the clouds of evil thickening over this Republic. The awful consequences are plain to be seen, by the aid of both ancient and modern history. Let him that readeth understand. But, O, for a Gideon, with his three hundred men, chosen of God, to go up against the towering walls of evil, and cause them to fall, forever fall, to rise no more.

A TREATISE

on the

INTELLECTUAL CHARACTER,

and Civil and Political Condition

of the

COLORED PEOPLE OF THE U. STATES;

and the

Prejudice Exercised towards Them:

With a Sermon

on the Duty of the Church

to Them

A TREATISE

ON THE

INTELLECTUAL CHARACTER,

AND

CIVIL AND POLITICAL CONDITION

OF THE

COLORED PEOPLE OF THE U. STATES;

AND THE

PREJUDICE EXERCISED TOWARDS THEM:

WITH A SERMON

ON THE

DUTY OF THE CHURCH TO THEM.

BY REV. H. EASTON,
A COLORED MAN.

BOSTON:
PRINTED AND PUBLISHED BY ISAAC KNAPP.

1837.

PREFACE.

IT IS WITH diffidence that I offer this treatise to the public; but an earnest desire to contribute my mite, for the benefit of my afflicted brethren, is my only apology. The subject is one of peculiar difficulty; especially as it is one in which I am deeply interested.

To speak or write on a subject relating to one's self, is peculiarly embarrassing; and especially so, under a deep sense of injury.

As an apology for the frequent errors that may occur in the following pages, I would remark: It cannot be reasonably expected, that a literary display could adorn the production of one from whom popular sentiment has withheld almost every advantage, even of a common education.

If this work should chance to fall into the hands of any whose minds are so sordid, and whose hearts are so inflexible, as to load it, with its author, with censure on that account merely, I would only say to them, that I shall not be disposed to envy them in the enjoyment of their sentiments, while I endeavor to content myself in the enjoyment of a consciousness of having done what I could to effect the establishment of righteousness and peace in the earth.

Hartford, Ct., March, 1837.

INTRODUCTION.

I CONCLUDE that, by this time, one great truth is acknowledged by all Christendom, *viz.*—God hath made of one blood all nations of men for to dwell on all the face of the earth. Or, in other words, I conclude it is a settled point with the wisest of the age, that no constitutional difference exists in the children of men, which can be said to be established by hereditary laws. If the proposition be granted, it will follow, that whatever differences exist, are casual or accidental. The variety of color, in the humun species, is the result of the same laws which variegate the whole creation. The same species of flowers is variegated with innumerable colors; and yet the species is the same, possessing the same general qualities, undergoing no intrinsic change, from these accidental causes. So it is with the human species. These varieties are indispensable, for the distinction of different objects, throughout the whole range of creation.

The hair is subject to the same laws of variety with the skin, though it may be considered in a somewhat different light. Were I asked why my hair is curled, my answer would be, because God gave nature the gift of producing variety, and that gift, like uncontrolled power every where, was desirous to act like itself; and thus being influenced by some cause unknown to man, she turned out her work in the form of my hair; and on being influenced by some other cause, she turned out hair of different texture, and gave it to another man. This would be the best answer I could give; for it is impossible for man to comprehend nature or her works. She has been supplied with an ability by her author to do wonders, insomuch that some have been foolish enough to think her to be God. All must confess she possesses a mysterious power to produce variety. We need only visit the potato and corn patch, (not a costly school,) and we shall be perfectly satisfied; for there, in the same hill, on one stalk, sprung from one potato, you may find several of different colors; and upon the same corn-stalk you may find two ears, one white or yellow, and the other deep red; and sometimes you may find an astonishing variety of colors displayed on one ear among the kernels; and what makes the observation more delightful, they are never found quarrelling about their color, though some have shades of extreme beauty. If you go to the field of grass, you will find that all grass is the same grass in variety; go to the herds and flocks, and among the feathered tribe, or view nature where you will, she tells us all that we can know, why it is that one man's head bears woolly, and another flaxen hair.

But when we come to talk about intellectual differences, we are brought into a new field of investigation. I call it a new or another field, because I cannot believe that nature has any thing to do in variegating intellect, any more than it has power over the soul. Mind can act on matter, but matter cannot act upon mind; hence it fills an entirely different sphere; therefore, we must look for a cause of difference of intellect elsewhere, for it cannot be found in nature. In looking for a cause, we have no right to go above nor below the sphere which the mind occupies; we cannot rationally conceive the cause to originate with God, nor in matter. Nature never goes out of her own limits to produce her works; all of which are perfect so far as she is concerned, and most assuredly God's works are perfect; hence, whatever imperfections there are in the mind, must have originated within its own sphere. But the question is, what is the cause and the manner it affects? Originally there was no difference of intellect, either constitutional or casual. Man was perfect, and therefore to him there was no exception. After he fell, we immediately find a difference of mind. In Abel we find characteristics of a noble soul, a prolific mind; his understanding appears to have been but very little, if any, impaired by the fall. But in Cain we find quite the reverse. His mind appears to have been narrow—his understanding dark—having wrapped himself up in a covetous mantle as contemptible as his conduct was wicked.

Now I see no reason why the causes of difference do not exist in the fall—in the act of transgression; for certain it is that the mind has since been subject to the influence of every species of evil, which must be a secondary cause to the existing effect. Or the subject may be viewed in the following light, viz.: evil and good exist in the world, and as the mind is influenced by the one or the other, so is the different effect produced thereby.

There is no truth more palpable than this, that the mind is capable of high cultivation; and that the degree of culture depends entirely on the means or agents employed to that end. In a country, therefore, where public sentiment is formed in favor of improving the mind, whatever the object may be, whether to promote good or evil, the mind is influenced thereby. The practical exercise of the mind is essential also to improvement and growth, and is directed likewise by public sentiment.

Public sentiment is founded on the real or imaginary interests of parties, whose individual interests are identified one with another. Public sentiment itself is directed in the exercise of its influence, by incidental circumstances, either local or foreign. In this current the mind is borne along, and at the instance of every change of event, is called to a new exercise of thought, conclusions, purposes, &c.; whereas, had it not been for the change, there would have been no action produced in the mind: for it is manifest, that the sphere which mankind are destined to fill, is surrounded with a great variety of acting laws, which, were it not for such causes, would make their minds entirely passive; but, under the influence of those causes, they are made to act not from constraint, but in accordance with an innate desire to avail themselves of collateral aid to their operations. It is manifest, therefore, that the more varying or complex the state of a people is incidentally rendered, the more power there is extant to call up renewed energies of the mind, the direct tendency of which is to confirm and strengthen it. Hence I deem it a fair conclusion, that whatever differences there are in the power of the intellect of nations, they are owing to the difference existing in the casual laws by which they are influenced. By consulting the history of nations, it may be seen that their genius perfectly accords with their habits of life, and the general maxims of their country; and that these habits and maxims possess a sameness of character with the incidental circumstances in which they originated.

As the intellect of a particular class will be in part the subject of this treatise, I wish in this place to follow the investigation of national difference of intellect, with its cause, by comparing the history of Europe and Africa.

Ham was the son of Noah, and founder of the African race, and progenitor to Assur, who probably founded the first government after the flood. It is evident from the best authority extant, that the arts and sciences flourished among this branch of the great family of man, long before its benefits were known to any other. History is explicit with regard to their hospitality also. At an early period of the existence of the government of Egypt, and while Chederlaomer, king of the Elamites, had already commenced the practice of robbery and bloodshed, Abraham was obliged by a famine to leave Canaan, where God had commanded him to settle, and to go into Egypt. 'This journey,' says a historian, 'gives occasion for Moses to mention some particulars with regard to the Egyptians; and every stroke discovers the character of an improved and powerful nation. The Egyptian monarch, and the grandeur of his court, are described in the most glowing colors;—and Ham, who let the colony into Egypt, has become the founder of a mighty empire. We are not, however, to imagine, that all the laws which took place in Egypt, and which have been so justly admired for their wisdom, were the work of this early age. Diodorus Siculus, a Greek writer, mentions many successive princes, who labored for their establishment and perfection. But in the time of Jacob, first principles of civil government seem to have been tolerably understood among the Egyptians. The country was divided into several districts or separate departments; councils, composed of experienced and select persons, were established for the management of public affairs; granaries for preserving corn were erected; and, in fine, the Egyptians in this age enjoyed a commerce far from inconsiderable. These facts, though of an ancient date, deserve our particular attention. It is from the Egyptians, that many of the arts, both of elegance and ability, have been handed down in an uninterrupted chain, to modern nations of Europe. The Egyptians communicated their arts to the Greeks; the Greeks taught the Romans many improvements, both in the arts of peace and war; and to the Romans, the present inhabitants of Europe are indebted for their civility and refinement.'

This noble people were not content with the enjoyment of luxury and ease, to the exclusion of their neighbors. At an early period they are found carrying the blessings of civilization into Greece; and, although repulsed in their first attempt by the rude barbarity of the Greeks, yet their philanthropy soon inspired them to resume the enterprise, which resulted in the settlement of two colonies, one in Argos, and the other in Attica. The founders of these colonies succeeded in their endeavors to unite the wandering Greeks, which laid a foundation for the instructions they afterwards gave them. Sesostris, a prince of wonderful ability, is supposed to mount the throne of Egypt about 2341 years before Christ. Egypt in his time, it is said, was in all probability the most powerful kingdom upon earth, and according to the best calculation, is supposed to contain twenty-seven millions of inhabitants. From the reign of Sesostris to that of Boccharis, a term of near 800 years, but little is known of the princes who reigned, but it is believed from collateral evidence, that the country in that time continued in a very flourishing condition, and for aught that is known, enjoyed uninterrupted peace. Wars and commotions, (says an eminent writer,) are the greatest themes of the historian, while the gentle and happy reign of a wise prince passes unobserved and unrecorded.

During this period of quietude at home, Egypt continued to pour forth her colonies into distant nations. Athens, that seat of learning and politeness, that school for all who aspired after wisdom, owes its foundation to Cecrops, who landed in Greece, with an Egyptian colony, before Christ 1585. The institutions which he established among the Athenians gave rise to the spread of the morals, arts and sciences in Greece, which have since shed their luster upon Rome, Europe, and America.

From the reign of Boccharis to the dissolution of their government, the Egyptians are celebrated for the wisdom of their laws and political institutions, which were dictated by the true spirit of civil wisdom. It appears that this race of people, during their greatest prosperity, made but very little proficiency in the art of war. We hear of but little of their conquests of armies, which is an evidence of their being an unwarlike people.

On taking a slight view of the history of Europe, we find a striking contrast. Javan, the third from Noah, and son of Japhet, is the stock from whom all the people known by the name of Greeks are descended. Javan established himself in the islands on the Western coast of Asia Minor. It is supposed, and it may not be impossible, that a few wanderers would escape over into Europe. Who would believe, says a writer, that the Greeks, who in latter ages became the patterns of politeness and every elegant art, were descended from a savage race of men, traversing the woods and wilds, inhabiting the rocks and caverns, a wretched prey to wild beasts and to one another. I would here remark that it is a little singular that modern philosophers, the descendants of this race of savages, should claim for their race a superiority of intellect over those who, at that very time, were enjoying all the real benefits of civilized life.

The remnant of this race which found their way to Europe from Asia Minor, are brought into notice but very little until after Rome had conquered the world. On the decline of that empire, from the death of Theodosius the great, A. D. 395 to A. D. 571, all Europe exhibited a picture of most melancholy Gothic barbarity. Literature, science, taste, were words scarce in use from this period to the sixteenth century. Persons of the highest rank could not read or write. Many of the clergy did not understand the learning which they were obliged daily to write; some of them could scarce read it.

The Goths and Vandals, and other fierce tribes, who were scattered over the vast countries of the North of Europe and Northwest of Asia, were drawn from their homes by a thirst for blood and plunder. Great bodies of armed men, with their wives and children, issued forth like regular colonies in quest of new settlements. New adventurers followed them. The lands which they deserted were occupied by more remote tribes of barbarians. These in their turn, pushed into more fertile countries, and like a torrent continually increasing, rolled on, and swept every thing before them.

Wherever the barbarians marched, their route was marked with blood. They ravaged or destroyed all around them. They made no distinction between what was sacred and what was profane. They respected no age, or sex, or rank. If man was called upon, (says an eminent historian,) to fix upon the period in the history of the world, during which the condition of the human race was most calamitous and afflicted, he would, without hesitation, name that which elapsed from A. D. 395 to 511. Cotemporary [sic] authors, who beheld that scene of destruction, labor and are at a loss for expressions to describe the horror of it. The scourge of God, the destroyer of nations, are the dreadful epithets by which they distinguish the most noted of the barbarous leaders.

Towards the close of the sixth century, the Saxons or Germans were masters of the Southern and more fertile provinces of Britain: the Franks, another tribe of Germans; the Goths of Spain; the Goths and Lombards of Italy, and the adjacent provinces.

During the period above mentioned, European slavery was introduced. Having, as yet, the art of navigation but very imperfectly, it seemed to be the whole bent of their mind to enslave each other.

A form of government, distinguished by the name of the Feudal system, was one under which the leaders of these barbarians became intolerable. They reduced the great body of them to actual servitude. They were slaves fixed to the soil, and with it transferred from one proprietor to another, by sale, or by conveyance. The kindred and dependants of an aggressor, as well as of a defender, were involved in a quarrel, without even the liberty of remaining neutral, whenever their superiors saw fit.

The king or general to whom they belonged, would lead them on to conquest, parcel out the land of the vanquished among his chief officers, binding those on whom they were bestowed, to follow his standard with a number of men, and to bear arms in his defence. The chief officers imitated the example of their sovereign, and in distributing portions of their lands among their dependents, annexed the same conditions to the grant.

For the smallest pretext they would make war with one another, and lead their slaves on to conquest; and take the land and goods of their foes as the reward of their enterprise. This system existed in the highlands in Scotland, as late as the year 1156.

It is not a little remarkable, that in the nineteenth century a remnant of this same barbarous people should boast of their national superiority of intellect, and of wisdom and religion; who, in the seventeenth century, crossed the Atlantic and practised the same crime their barbarous ancestry had done in the fourth, fifth and sixth centuries: bringing with them the same boasted spirit of enterprise; and not unlike their fathers, staining their route with blood, as they have rolled along, as a cloud of locusts, towards the West. The late unholy war with the Indians, and the wicked crusade against the peace of Mexico, are striking illustrations of the nobleness of this race of people, and the powers of their mind. I will here take a brief review of the events following each race from their beginning.

Before Christ 2188, Misraim, the son of Ham, founded the kingdom of Egypt, which lasted 1633 years.

2059, Ninus, the son of Belus, another branch of Ham's family, founds the kingdom of Assyria, which lasted 1000 years, and out of its ruins Babylon, Ninevah, and the kingdom of the Medes.

1822, Memnon, the Egyptian, invents the letters.

1571, Moses born in Egypt, and adopted by Pharaoh's daughter, who educated him in all the learning of the Egyptians.

1556, Cecrops brings a colony from Egypt into Attica, and begins the kingdom of Athens, in Greece.

1485, The first ship that appeared in Greece was brought from Egypt by Danaus, who arrived at Rhodes, and brought with him his fifty daughters.

869, The city of Carthage, in Africa, founded by queen Dido.

604, By order of Necho, king of Egypt, some Phenicians, sailed from the Red Sea round Africa, and returned by the Mediterranean.

600, Thales, of Miletus, travels to Egypt, to acquire the knowledge of geometry, astronomy, and philosophy; returns to Greece and calculates eclipses, gives general notions of the universe, &c.

285, Dionysius, of Alexandria, began his astronomical era, on Monday, June 26, being the first who found the exact solar year to consist of 365 days, 5 hours, and 49 minutes.

284, Ptolemy Philadelphus, king of Egypt, employs seventy-two interpreters to translate the Old Testament into the Greek language, which was called the Septuagint.

237, Hamilcar, the Carthagenian, causes his son Hannibal, at nine years of age, to swear eternal enmity to the Romans.

218, Hannibal passes the Alps, at the age of 28 years, and defeats the Romans in several battles.

47, The Alexandrian library, consisting of 400,000 valuable books burned by accident.

30, Alexandria is taken by Octavius, upon which Mark Antony and Cleopatra, put themselves to death, and Egypt is reduced to a Roman province.

640, A. D., Alexandria is taken by the Saracens, or followers of Mahomet, and the grand library burned by order of Omar, their caliph or prince.

991, The figures in arithmetic are brought into Europe by the Saracens from Arabia. [Poor negroes, I wonder where they got learning.

These are the race of people who are charged with an inferiority of intellect.]

Africa could once boast of several states of eminence, among which are Egypt, Ethiopia, and Carthage; the latter supported an extensive commerce, which was extended to every part of the then known world. Her fleets even visited the British shores, and was every where prosperous, until she was visited with the scourge of war, which opened the way for those nations whose life depended on plunder. The Romans have the honor, by the assistance of the Mauritonians, of subduing Carthage; after which the North of Africa was overrun by the Vandals, who, in their march destroyed all arts and sciences; and, to add to the calamity of this quarter of the world, the Saracens made a sudden conquest of all the coasts of Egypt and Barbary, in the seventh century. And these were succeeded by the Turks, both being of the Mahomedan religion, whose professors carried desolation wherever they went; and thus the ruin of that once flourishing part of the world was completed. Since that period, Africa has been robbed of her riches and honor, and sons and daughters, to glut the rapacity of the great minds of European bigots.

The following is a short chronological view of the events following the rise of the Europeans.

A. D. 49, London is founded by the Romans.

51, Caractacus, the British king is carried in chains to Rome.

59, Nero persecutes the Druids in Britain.

61, The British queen defeats the Romans, but is conquered soon after by Suetonius, governor of Britain.

63, Christianity introduced into Britain.

85, Julius Agricola, governor of South Britain, to protect the civilized Britons from the incursions of the Caledonians, builds a line of forts between the rivers Forth and Clyde; defeats the Caledonians; and first sails round Britain, which he discovers to be an island.

222, About this time the barbarians begin their eruptions and the Goths have annual tribute not to molest the Roman government.

274, The art of manufacturing silk first introduced into Britain from India; the manufacturing of it introduced into Europe by some monks, 551.

404, The kingdom of Caledonia, or Scotland, revives under Fergus.

406, The Vandals, Alans, and Suevi spread in France and Spain, by a concession of Honorius, emperor of the West.

410, Rome taken and plundered by Alaric, king of visi-Goths.

412, The Vandals begin their kingdom in Spain.

446, The Romans having left the Britons to themselves, are greatly harassed by the Scots and Picts, they make their complaints to Rome again, which they entitle, the groans of the Britons.

449, The Saxons join the Britons against the Scots and Picts.

455, Saxons having repulsed the Scots and Picts begin to establish themselves in Kent under Hengist.

476, Several new states arise in Italy and other parts, consisting of Goths, Vandals, Huns, and other barbarians, under whom literature is extinguished, and the works of the learned are destroyed.

496, Clovis, king of France, baptized, and Christianity begins in that kingdom.

508, Prince Arthur begins his reign over the Britons.

609, Here begins the power of the Pope by the concession of Phocas, emperor of the east.

685, The Britons, after a struggle of near 150 years, are totally expelled by the Saxons, and drove into Wales and Cornwall.

712, The Saracens conquer Spain.

726, The controversy about images occasions many insurrections.

800, Charlemagne, king of France, begins the empire of Germany, and endeavors to restore learning.

838, The Scots and Picts have a hard fight. The former prevail.

867, The Danes begin their ravages in England.

896, Alfred the Great fought 56 battles with the invading Danes, after which he divides his kingdom into counties, hundreds, tythings; erect courts: and founds the University of Oxford.

936, The Saracen empire is divided into seven kingdoms, by usurpation.

1015, Children forbidden by law to be sold by their parents, in England.

1017, Canute, king of Denmark, gets possession of England.

1040, The Danes after much hard fighting are driven out of Scotland.

1041, The Saxon line restored under Edward.

1043, The Turks who had hitherto fought for other nations, have become formidable, and take possession of Persia.

1059, Malcolm III, king of Scotland, kills Macbeth, and marries the princess Margaret.

1065, The Turks take Jerusalem.

1066, The conquest of England by William; who

1070, introduced the feudal law.

1075, Henry IV, emperor of Germany, and the Pope, have a quarrel. Henry, in penance walks barefoot in January.

1096, The first crusade to the Holy Land is begun, under several Christian princes, to drive the infidels from Jerusalem.

1118, The order of knight templars instituted.

1172, Henry II, king of England, takes possession of Ireland.

1182, Pope Alexander III, compels the kings of France and England, to hold the stirrups of his saddle when he mounted his horse.

1192, Richard, king of England, defeats Saladin's army, consisting of 300,000 combatants.

1200, Chimnies not known in England.

1227, The Tartars emerge from the Northern part of Asia, and in imitation of former conquerers, carry death and desolation wherever they march. They overrun all the Saracen empire.

1233, The inquisition began in 1204, is now in the hands of the Dominicans.

1258, The Tartars take Bagdad, which finishes the empire of the Saracens.

1263, Acho, king of Norway, invades Scotland with 160 sail, and lands 20,000 men at the mouth of the Clyde, who were cut to pieces by Alexander III.

1273, The empire of the present Austrian family begins in Germany.

1282, Lewellyn, prince of Wales, defeated and killed by Edward I, who unites that principality to England.

1314, Battle between Edward II, and Robert Bruce, which establishes the latter on the throne of Scotland.

1340, Gunpowder and guns first invented by Swartz. 1346, Bombs and four pieces of cannon were made, by which Edward III gained the battle of Cressy.

1346, The battle of Durham, in which David, king of Scots, is taken prisoner.

1356, The battle of Poictiers, in which king John of France and his son are taken prisoners by Edward, the black prince.

1362, John Wickliffe calls in question the doctrines of the church of Rome, whose followers are called Lollards.

1388, The battle of Otterburn between Hotspur and the Earl of Douglas.

1415, Battle gained over the French by Henry V of England.

1428, The siege of Orleans.

1453, Constantinople taken by the Turks.

1483, Civil war ended between the house of York and Lancaster, after a siege of 30 years, and the loss of 100,000 men.

1489, Maps and sea charts first brought to England.

1492, America first discovered by Columbus.

1494, Algebra first known in Europe.

1497, South America first discovered.

1499, North America by Cabot.

1517, Martin Luther begins the reformation.

1616, The first permanent settlement in Virginia.

1621, New England planted by the Puritans.

1635, Province of Maryland planted by Lord Baltimore.

1640, The massacre in Ireland, when 40,000 English protestants are killed.

1649, Charles I beheaded.

1664, The New Netherlands in North America, taken from the Swedes and Dutch by the English.

1667, The peace of Breda, which confirms to the English the New Netherlands, now known by names of Pennsylvania, New York, and New Jersey.

The object I have in introducing this account of events, attendant on the rise and progress of the African and European nations, is, that the traits of their national character may at a glance be discovered; by which the reader may the better judge of the superiority of the descendants of Japhet over those of Ham. In the first place, the European branch of Japhet's family have but very little claims to the rank of civilized nations. From the fourth up to the sixteenth century, they were in the deepest state of heathenish barbarity. A continual scene of bloodshed and robbery was attendant on the increase of their numbers. Their spread over different countries caused almost an entire extinction of all civil and religious governments, and of the liberal arts and sciences. And ever since that period, all Europe and America have been little else than one great universal battle field.

It is true, there is a great advance in the arts and sciences from where they once were; but whether they are any where near its standard, as they once existed in Africa, is a matter of strong doubt. We should without doubt, had not the Europeans destroyed every vestige of history, which fell in their barbarous march, been favored with an extensive and minute history of the now unknown parts of Africa. Certain it is, however, that whatever they may have contributed of knowledge to the world, it is owing to these casual circumstances we have mentioned, rather than any thing peculiar to them as a people.

Any one who has the least conception of true greatness, on comparing the two races by means of what history we have, must decide in favor of the descendants of Ham. The Egyptians alone have done more to cultivate such improvements as comports to the happiness of mankind, than all the descendants of Japhet put together. Their enterprise in establishing colonies and governments among their barbarous neighbors, and supplying their wants from their granaries,

instead of taking the advantage of their ignorance, and robbing them
of what little they had, does not look much like an inferiority of intellect, nor a want of disposition to make a proper use of it. They, at no
age, cultivated the art of war to any great extent. Neither are they
found making an aggressive war with any nation. But while other
nations were continually robbing and destroying each other, they
were cultivating internal improvement; and virtually became a store-
house of every thing conducive to the happiness of mankind, with
which she supplied their wants. Even as late as Carthage was in her
glory, that race of people exhibited their original character. For that
famed city never acquired its greatness, but by the cultivation of commerce. And though she obtained command of both sides of the Mediterranean, became mistress of the sea, made the islands of Corsica
and Sardinia tributary to her, yet it is evident she acquired this advantage by her wealth, rather than by her arms.

Europe and America presents quite a different spectacle. There is
not a foot of God's earth which is now occupied by them, but has been
obtained, in effect, by the dint of war, and the destruction of the vanquished, since the founding of London, A. D. 49. Their whole career
presents a motley mixture of barbarism and civilization, of fraud and
philanthropy, of patriotism and avarice, of religion and bloodshed.
And notwithstanding many great and good men have lived and died
bright luminaries of the world—and notwithstanding there are many
now living who are the seed of the church, yet it must be admitted that
almost every nation in Europe, and especially Americans, retain, in
principle, if not in manners, all the characteristics of their barbarous
and avaricious ancestors. And instead of their advanced state in science being attributable to a superior developement of intellectual
faculties, there is nothing more capable of proof, than that it is solely
owing to the nature of the circumstances into which they were drawn
by their innate thirst for blood and plunder.

Had the inhabitants of Egypt, Ethiopia, Carthage, and other kingdoms in Africa, been possessed with the same disposition, the probability is, that the world now would be in a heathenish darkness, for the

want of that information which their better disposition has been capable of producing. And had they had the means at that early age of understanding human nature, as they now would have, were their kingdoms in their glory, they would probably not have suffered their liberality to be taken advantage of by a barbarous crew around them. It is not for the want of mind, therefore, that Africa is in her present state; for were the dispositions of her different nations like the ancient barbarians of Europe, they would soon make a plenty of business for Europeans, with all their advantages, to defend themselves against their depredations. But it is not the genius of the race. Nothing but liberal, generous principles, can call the energies of an African mind into action. And when these principles are overruled by a foreign cause, they are left without any thing to inspire them to action, other than the cravings of their animal wants.

Africa never will raise herself, neither will she be raised by others, by warlike implements, or ardent spirits; nor yet by a hypocritical religious crusade, saying one thing and meaning another. But when she rises, other nations will have learned to deal justly with her from principle. When that time shall arrive, the lapse of a few generations will show the world that her sons will again take the lead in the field of virtuous enterprise, filling the front ranks of the church, when she marches into the millennial era.

CHAPTER I.

On the Intellectual Character of the Colored People of these United States of America.

In this country we behold the remnant of a once noble, but now heathenish people. In calling the attention of my readers to the subject which I here present them, I would have them lose sight of the African character, about which I have made some remarks in my introduction. For at this time, circumstances have established as much difference between them and their ancestry, as exists between them and any other race or nation. In the first place the colored people who are born in this country, are Americans in every sense of the word. Americans by birth, genius, habits, language, &c. It is supposed, and I think not without foundation, that the slave population labor under an intellectual and physical disability or inferiority. The justness of these conclusions, however, will apply only to such as have been subject to slavery some considerable length of time.

I have already made some remarks with regard to the cause of apparent differences between nations. I shall have cause to remark again, that as the intellectual as well as the physical properties of mankind, are subject to cultivation, I have observed that the growth or culture depends materially on the means employed to that end. In those countries in which the maxims and laws are such as are calculated to employ the physical properties mostly, such as racing, hunting, &c., there is uniformly a full development of physical properties.

We will take the American Indian for example. A habit of indolence produces a contrary effect. History, as well as experience, will justify me in saying that a proper degree of exercise is essential to the growth of the corporeal system; and that the form and size depends on the extent and amount of exercise. On comparing one who is brought up from his youth a tradesman, with one who is brought up a farmer, the difference is manifestly apparent according to the difference of their exercise. Change of public sentiment indirectly affects the form and size of whole nations, inasmuch as public sentiment dictates the mode and kind of exercise. The muscular yeomanry who once formed a majority of our country's population, are now but seldom found; those who fill their places in society, in no way compare with them in that respect. Compare our farmer's daughters, who have been brought up under the influence of country habits, with those brought up under city habits, and a difference is most manifest.

But there is another consideration worthy of notice. Education, says D. D. Hunter,* on the part of the mother, commences from the moment she has the prospect of being a mother. And her own health thenceforth is the first duty she owes to her child. The instructions given to the wife of Manoah, and mother of Sampson, the Nazarite, (Jud. 13, 4:) 'Now, therefore, beware, I pray thee, drink not wine nor strong drink, and eat not any unclean thing,' are not merely arbitrarily adapted only to a particular branch of political economy, and intended to serve local and temporary purposes; no, the constitutions of nature, reason, and experience, which unite in recommending to those who have the prospect of being mothers, a strict attention to diet, to exercise, to temper, to every thing, which affecting the frame of their own body or mind, may communicate an important, a lasting, perhaps indelible impression, to the mind or body of their offspring. A proper regimen for themselves, is therefore the first stage of education for their children. The neglect of it is frequently found productive of effects which no future culture is able to alter or rectify.

*Hunter's Sacred Biography, vol. 7. page 10.

These most just remarks confirm me in the opinion, that the laws of nature may be crossed by the misconduct or misfortune of her who has the prospect of being a mother. Apply these remarks to the condition of slave mothers, as such, and what are the plain and natural inferences to be drawn. Certainly, if they are entitled to any weight at all, the intellectual and physical inferiority of the slave population can be accounted for without imputing it to an original hereditary cause. Contemplate the exposed condition of slave mothers—their continual subjection to despotism and barbarity; their minds proscribed to the narrow bounds of servile obedience, subject to irritation from every quarter; great disappointment, and physical suffering themselves, and continual eye-witnesses to maiming and flagellation; shrieks of woe borne to their ears on every wind. Indeed, language is lame in the attempt to describe the condition of those poor daughters of affliction. Indeed, I have no disposition to dwell on the subject; to be obliged to think of it at all, is sufficiently harrowing to my feelings. But I would inquire how it can be possible for nature, under such circumstances, to act up to her perfect laws?

The approbrious terms used in common by most all classes, to describe the deformities of the offspring of these parents, is true in part, though employed with rather bad grace by those in whom the cause of their deformity originates. I will introduce those terms, not for the sake of embellishing my treatise with their modest style, but to show the lineal effects of slavery on its victims. Contracted and sloped foreheads; prominent eye-balls; projecting under-jaw; certain distended muscles about the mouth, or lower parts of the face; thick lips and flat nose; hips and rump projecting; crooked shins; flat feet, with large projecting heels. This, in part, is the language used by moderns to philosophize, upon the negro character. With regard to their mind, it is said that their intellectual brain is not fully developed; malicious disposition; no taste for high and honorable attainments; implacable enemies one to another; and that they sustain the same relation to the ourang outang, that the whites do to them.

Now, as it respects myself, I am perfectly willing to admit the truth of these remarks, as they apply to the character of a slave population; for I am aware that no language capable of being employed by mortal tongue, is sufficiently descriptive to set forth in its true character the effect of that cursed thing, slavery. I shall here be under the necessity of calling up those considerations connected with the subject, which I but a little time since entertained a hope that I should be able to pass by unnoticed; I have reference to a mother who is a slave, bringing into the world beings whose limbs and minds were lineally fashioned for the yoke and fetter, long before her own immortal mind was clothed in materiality.

I would ask my readers to think of woman as the greatest natural gift to man—think of her in delicate health, when the poor delicate fabric is taxed to the utmost to answer the demands of nature's laws—when friends and sympathies, nutricious [*sic*] aliments, and every other collateral aid is needed. O think of poor woman, a prospective mother; and when you think, feel as a heart of flesh can feel; see her weeping eyes fixed alternately upon the object of her affections and him who accounts her a brute—think how she feels on beholding the gore streaming from the back, the naked back, of the former, while the latter wields the accursed lash, until the back of a husband, indeed the whole frame, has become like a loathsome heap of mangled flesh. How often has she witnessed the wielding club lay him prostrate, while the purple current followed the damning blow. How the rattling of the chain, the lock of which has worn his ankles and his wrists to the bone, falls upon her ear. O, has man fallen so far below the dignity of his original character, as not to be susceptible of feeling. But does the story stop here. I would that it were even so. But alas! this, the ornamental production of nature's God, is not exempt, even in this state, from the task of a slave. And, as though cursed by all the gods, her own delicate frame is destined to feel the cruel scourge. When faint and weary she lags her step, the overseer, as though decreed to be a tormenting devil, throws the coiling lash upon her naked back; and in turn, the master makes it his pleasure to despoil the works of God, by subjecting her to the rank of goods and chattels, to be sold in the shambles. Woman, you who possess a woman's nature, can feel for her who was destined by the Creator of you both, to fill the same sphere with yourself. You know by experience the claims of nature's laws—you know too well the irritability of your natures when taxed to the utmost to fulfill the decree of nature's God.

I have in part given a description of a mother that is a slave. And can it be believed to be possible for such a one to bring perfect children into the world. If we are permitted to decide that natural causes produce natural effects, then it must be equally true that unnatural causes produce unnatural effects. The slave system is an unnatural cause, and has produced its unnatural effects, as displayed in the deformity of two and a half millions of beings, who have been under its soul-and-body-destroying influence, lineally, for near three hundred years; together with all those who have died their progenitors since that period.

But again, I believe it to be an axiom generally admitted, that mind acts on matter, then again, that mind acts on mind; this being the case, is it a matter of surprise that those mothers who are slaves, should, on witnessing the distended muscles on the face of whipped slaves, produce the same or similar distensions on the face of her offspring, by her own mind being affected by the sight; and so with all other deformities. Like causes produce like effects. If by Jacob's placing ring-streaked elder in the trough where Laban's flocks drank, caused their young to be ring-streaked and speckled, why should not the offspring of slave mothers, who are continually witnessing exciting objects, be affected by the same law; and why should they not be more affected, as the mother is capable of being more excited.

From the foregoing I draw the following conclusions, with regard to the different degrees of effect produced by slavery. Compare slaves that are African born, with those who are born in slavery, and the latter will in no wise compare with the former in point of form of person or strength of mind. The first and second generation born in this country are generally far before the fourth and fifth, in this respect. Compare such as have been house servants, as they are called,

for several generations with such as have been confined to planta-
tions the same term of time, and there will be a manifest inferiority in
the latter. Observe among the nominally free, their form of person,
features, strength of mind, and bent of genius, fidelity, &c., and it will
evidently appear that they who sustain a relation of no further than
the third generation from African birth, are in general far before
those who sustain a more distant relation. The former generally acquire small possessions, and conform their habits of life and modes of
operation with those common where they live, while those who have
been enslaved for several generations, or whose progenitors in direct
line were thus enslaved, cannot be induced to conform to any regular
rule of life or operation. I intend this last statement as general fact, of
which, however, there are exceptions; where there is a mixture of
blood, as it is sometimes called, perhaps these remarks may not apply. I suppose, however, that in case of a union between a degraded
American slave of the last order spoken of, and a highly intelligent
free American, whether white or colored, that the offspring of such
parents are as likely to partake of the influence of slavery through the
lineal medium of the slave parent, as to receive natural intelligence
through the medium of the other.

So far as I understand, nature's law seems not to be scrupulously
rigid in this particular: there appears to be no rule, therefore, by
which to determine the effect or lineal influence of slavery on a mixed
race. I am satisfied with regard to one fact, however, that caste has no
influence whatever: for a union between a highly cultivated black and
a degraded one, produces an exact similar effect. Whatever complexion or nation parents thus connected may be of, the effect produced
would be the same, but it would not be certain that their children
would occupy a midway region between the intelligent and degraded
parent, as in other cases part of a family may be below mediocrity,
and part above, in point of form and intellect. One thing is certain,
which may have some bearing in the case; that when nature has been
robbed, give her a fair chance and she will repair her loss by her own
operations, one of which is to produce variety. But to proceed further

with any remarks on this point, I feel myself not at liberty. In view of what I have said on this subject, I am aware of having fallen short of giving a full description of the lineal influence and effects slavery has upon the colored population of this country. Such is the nature of the subject, that it is almost impossible to arrange our thoughts so as to follow it by any correct rule of investigation.

Slavery, in its effects, is like that of a complicated disease, typifying evil in all its variety—in its operations, omnipotent to destroy—in effect, fatal as death and hell. Language is lame in its most successful attempt, to describe its enormity; and with all the excitement which this country has undergone, in consequence of the discussion of the subject, yet the story is not half told, neither can it be. We, who are subject to its fatal effects, cannot fully realize the disease under which we labor. Think of a colored community, whose genius and temperament of minds all differ in proportion as they are lineally or personally made to feel the damning influence of slavery, and, as though it had the gift of creating tormenting pangs at pleasure, it comes up, in the character of an accuser, and charges our half destroyed, discordant minds, with hatred one towards the other, as though a body composed of parts, and systematized by the laws of nature, were capable of continuing its regular configurative movements after it has been decomposed.

When I think of nature's laws, that with scrupulous exactness they are to be obeyed by all things over which they are intended to bear rule, in order that she may be able to declare, in all her variety, that the hand that made her is divine, and when, in this case, I see and feel how she has been robbed of her means to perform her delightful task—her laws trampled under feet with all their divine authority, despoiling her works even in her most sacred temples—I wonder that I am a man; for though of the third generation from slave parents, yet in body and mind nature has never been permitted to half finish her work. Let all judge who is in the fault, God, or slavery, or its sustainers?

CHAPTER II.

On the Political Condition and Character of the
Colored People.

A GOVERNMENT like this is at any time liable to be revolutionized by the people, at any and every time there is a change of public sentiment. This, perhaps, is as it should be. But when the subjects of a republican government become morally and politically corrupt, there is but little chance remaining for republicanism. A correct standard may be set up, under which parties may pretend to aim at a defence of the original principles upon which the government was based; but if the whole country has become corrupt, what executive power is there remaining to call those parties in question, and to decide whether their pretensions and acts correspond with the standard under which they profess to act. Suppose the Constitution and articles of confederation, be the admitted correct standard by all parties, still the case is no better, when there is not honesty enough in either, to admit a fair construction of their letter and spirit. Good laws, and a good form of government, are of but very little use to a wicked people, further than they are able to restrain them from wickedness.

Were a fallen angel permitted to live under the government of heaven, his disposition would first incline him to explain away the nature of its laws; this done, their spirit becomes perverted, which places him back in hell from whence he came; for, though he could not alter the laws of heaven, yet he could pervert their use, in himself, and act them out in this perverted state, which would make him act just like a devil. The perversion of infinite good, is infinite evil—and if the spiritual use of the laws of an infinitely perfect government is productive of a perfect heaven, in like manner their spiritual perversion is productive of perfect or infinite hell. Hence it is said to be a bottomless pit—ay, deep as the principle is high, from which the distortion is made.

I have taken this course to illustrate the state of a people with a good government and laws, and with a disposition to explain away all their meaning. My conclusions are, that such republicans are capable, like the angel about which I have spoken, to carry out their republicanism into the most fatal despotism. A republican form of government, therefore, can be a blessing to no people, further than they make honest virtue the rule of life. Indeed, honesty is essential to the existence of a republican form of government, for it originates in a contract or agreement of its subjects, relative to the disposal of their mutual interests. If conspiracy is got up by any of the contracters, against the fundamental principles of the honest contract, (which, if republican, embraced those interests which are unalienable, and no more,) and if, by an influence gained by them, so as to make its intent null and void, the foundation of the government is thereby destroyed; leaving its whole fabric a mere wreck, inefficient in all its executive power. Or if the contract had the form of honesty only, when there was a secret design of fraud in the minds of the parties contracting, then of course, it is a body without a soul—a fabric without a foundation; and, like a dead carcass entombed, will tumble to pieces as soon as brought to the light of truth, and into the pure air of honesty.

With regard to the claims of the colored subjects of this government to equal political rights, I maintain that their claims are founded in an original agreement of the contracting parties, and that there is nothing to show that color was a consideration in the agreement. It is well known that when the country belonged to Great Britain, the colored people were slaves. But when America revolted from Britain, they were held no longer by any legal power. There was no efficient law in the land except marshal law, and that regarded no one as a slave. The inhabitants were governed by no other law, except by resolutions adopted from time to time by meetings convoked in the different colonies. Upon the face of the warrants by which these district and town meetings were called, there is not a word said about the color of the attendants. In convoking the continental Congress of the 4th of September, 1776, there was not a word said about color. In November of the same year, Congress met again, to get in readiness twelve thousand men to act in any emergency; at the same time, a request was forwarded to Connecticut, New Hampshire, and Rhode Island, to increase this army to twenty thousand men. Now it is well known that hundreds of the men of which this army was composed, were colored men, and recognized by Congress as Americans.

An extract from the speech of Richard Henry Lee, delivered in Congress, assembled June 8, 1776, in support of a motion, which he offered, to declare America free and independent, will give some view of the nature of the agreement upon which this government is based. 'The eyes of all Europe are fixed upon us; she demands of us a living example of freedom, that may contrast, by the felicity of her citizens, (I suppose black as well as white,) with the ever increasing tyranny which desolates her polluted shores. She invites us to prepare an asylum where the unhappy may find solace, and the persecuted, repose. She entreats us to cultivate a propitious soil, where that generous plant which first sprang up and grew in England, but is now withered by the poisonous blasts of Scottish tyranny, may revive and flourish, sheltering under its salubrious and interminable shade all the unfortunate of the human race.'

The principles which this speech contains, are manifestly those which were then acted upon. To remove all doubt on this point, I will make a short extract from the Declaration of Independence, in Congress assembled, fourth of July, 1776. 'We, the representatives of these United States of America, in general Congress assembled, appealing to the Supreme Judge of the world for the rectitude of our intentions, and by the authority of the good people of these Colonies, solemnly publish and declare, that these united colonies are, and of right ought to be, free and independent States. (And now for the pledge.) We mutually pledge to each other our lives, our fortunes, and our sacred honor.' The representatives who composed that Congress were fifty-five in number, and all signed the declaration and pledge in behalf of the good people of the thirteen States.

Now I would ask, can it be said, from any fair construction of the foregoing extracts, that the colored people are not recognized as citizens? Congress drew up articles of confederation also, among which are found the following reserved state privileges. 'Each state has the exclusive right of regulating its internal government, and of framing its own laws, in all matters not included in the articles of confederation, and which are not repugnant to it.' Another article reads as follows: 'There shall be a public treasury for the service of the confederation, to be replenished by the particular contributions of each state, the same to be proportioned according to the number of inhabitants of every age, sex, or condition, with the exception of Indians.'

These extracts are sufficient to show the civil and political recognition of the colored people. In addition to which, however, we have an official acknowledgment of their equal, civil, and political relation to the government, in the following proclamation of Major General Andrew Jackson, to the colored people of Louisiana, Sept. 21, 1814; also of Thomas Butler, Aid[e] de Camp:

'*Head Quarters, Seventh Military District, Mobile, September* 21, 1814. *To the Free Colored Inhabitants of Louisiana.*

'Through a mistaken policy you have heretofore been deprived of a participation in the glorious struggle for national rights, in which our country is engaged. This no longer shall exist.

'As sons of Freedom, you are now called upon to defend our most inestimable blessing. As Americans, your country looks with confidence to her adopted children, for a valorous support, as a faithful return for the advantages enjoyed under her mild and equitable government. As fathers, husbands, and brothers, you are summoned to rally round the standard of the Eagle, to defend all which is dear in existence.

'Your country, although calling for your exertions, does not wish you to engage in her cause, without remunerating you for the services rendered. Your intelligent minds are not to be led away by false representations—your love of honor would cause you to despise the man who should attempt to deceive you. In the sincerity of a soldier, and the language of truth, I address you.

'To every noble hearted free man of color, volunteering to serve during the present contest with Great Britain and no longer, there will be paid the same bounty in money and lands, now received by the white soldiers of the United States, viz., one hundred and twenty-four dollars in money, and one hundred and sixty acres of land. The non-commissioned officers and privates will also be entitled to the same monthly pay and daily rations and clothes, furnished to any American soldier.

'On enrolling yourselves in companies, the Major General commanding, will select officers for your government, from your white fellow citizens. Your non-commissioned officers will be appointed from among yourselves.

'Due regard will be paid to the feelings of freemen and soldiers. You will not, by being associated with white men in the same corps, be exposed to improper comparisons or unjust sarcasm. As a distinct, independent battalion or regiment, pursuing the path of glory, you will, undivided, receive the applause and gratitude of your countrymen.

'To assure you of the sincerity of my intentions, and my anxiety to engage your invaluable services to our country, I have communicated my wishes to the Governor of Louisiana, who is fully informed as to the manner of enrolments, and will give you every necessary information on the subject of this address.

'ANDREW JACKSON, *Major General Commanding.*' '*Proclamation to the Free People of Color.*

'Soldiers!—When on the banks of the Moble, I called you to take arms, inviting you to partake the perils and glory of your white fellow citizens, *I expected much from you;* for I was not ignorant that you possessed qualities most formidable to an invading enemy. I knew with what fortitude you could endure hunger and thirst, and all the fatigues of a campaign. *I knew well how you loved your native country,* and that you had, as well as ourselves, to defend what man holds most dear—his parents, relations, wife, children and property: *You have done more than I expected.* In addition to the previous qualities I before knew you to possess, I found moreover, among you, a noble enthusiasm which leads to the performance of great things.

'Soldiers!—The President of the United States shall hear how praiseworthy was your conduct in the hour of danger, and the representatives of the American people will, I doubt not, give you the praise your exploits entitle you to. Your General anticipates them in applauding your noble ardor.

'The enemy approaches, his vessels cover our lakes; our brave citizens are united, and all contention has ceased among them. Their only dispute is, who shall win the prize of valor, or who the most glory, its noblest reward.

'By Order, THOMAS BUTLER, *Aide de Camp.*'

All the civil and political disabilities of the colored people, are the effect of usurpation. It is true, slavery is recognized by the articles of confederation; but there is not a public document of the government, which recognizes a colored man as a slave, not even in the provision for Southern representation.

When fugitive slaves are demanded by Southern slaveholders, they are recovered by virtue of a provision made to recover prisoners held to labor, in the state from whence they have absconded; but how that provision can be construed in such a manner, as to give them that advantage, I cannot conceive. I am satisfied, that it only serves as a pretext to justify a base perversion of the law, for the sake of pleasing evil doers. In the first place, a slave is not held to labor legally in slave states, because, according to the extract I have made, viz., that each state has a right to frame laws which are not *prejudicial* to the articles of confederation; there is a limitation to which every other article of the document is subject. Now, what says another article of confederation? Why, that a person held to labor, shall be recovered. But in what way held? Upon this the articles of confederation, are silent; in fact, they may as well be silent; for had they pointed out the manner of persons being held to labor, they would have assumed the province of common law; this, the framers of the constitution and documents of confederation, knew full well; and the administrators of justice now know, that no person under heaven can be held to labor, other than by virtue of a contract, recognizable by common law. Neither do the administrators of justice, found their decisions on any thing found in the articles of confederation; for a proof of which, I will call the attention of my readers to the following considerations.

If a white person is arraigned before a justice, as a fugitive slave, it would not be all the evidence that could be collected to prove him a slave, however true, that would induce a justice at the North to give him up, if he were able to prove that he was of white parentage. It would be the same, in case that an Indian was arraigned. There have been such claims made, I believe, and the defendants acquitted, even where there was proof positive, on the part of the claimant. This is proof positive, that decisions in such cases are not founded on a sentence contained in the articles of confederation, for there is nothing said, in that instrument, about nation or complexion; but persons held to labor. Now, if it is by virtue of that instrument, that the black man is held to labor, why not hold the white person, and the Indian, by the same power? And if they cannot be held by that instrument, how can any person be held, when no particular person is described? It is evident that decisions in favor of claimants are founded in the fact of the defendants being a black person, or descendants of blacks or Africans. Now, for all this mode of administering justice, there cannot be found a single sentence of justification, in any public document in the country, except such as have been framed by individual states; and these are prejudicial to the articles of confederation. If there is any thing in the articles of confederation, which justifies such a course of procedure, I have never found it. Only think, if one is claimed who is black, or who is a descendant of a black, (though he be whiter than a white man,) he must be given up to hopeless bondage, by virtue of the articles of confederation, when there is not a word about *black* contained in the instrument; whereas, if a white person be claimed, if he is half negro, if he can prove himself legally white, or of white parentage, he is acquitted. This course of conduct would be scouted by heathens, as a gross libel upon humanity and justice. It is so; and a violation of the Constitution, and of the Bill of Rights—the rights of the people; and every State which connives at such robbing in high places, clothed with a legal form, without a vestige of legal authority; and that too, are having taken the tremendous *oath,* as recorded in the Declaration of Independence, ought to have *perjury* written upon their statute books, and upon the ceiling of their legislative halls, in letters as large as their crime, and as black as the complexion of the injured.

Excuses have been employed in vain to cover up the hypocrisy of this nation. The most corrupt policy which ever disgraced its barbarous ancestry, has been adopted by both church and state, for the avowed purpose of withholding the *inalienable rights* of one part of the subjects of the government. Pretexts of the lowest order, which are neither witty or decent, and which rank among that order of subterfuges, under which the lowest of ruffians attempt to hide, when exposed to detection, are made available. Indeed, I may say in candor, that a highwayman or assassin acts upon principles far superior, in some respects, in comparison with those under which the administrators of the laws of church and state act, especially in their attempts to hide themselves and their designs from the just censure of the world, and from the burning rays of truth. I have no language to express what I see, and hear, and feel, on this subject. Were I capable of dipping my pen in the deepest dye of crime, and of understanding the science of the bottomless pit, I should then fail in presenting to the intelligence of mortals on earth, the true nature of American deception. There can be no appeals made in the name of the laws of the country, of philanthropy, or humanity, or religion, that is capable of drawing forth any thing but the retort,—*you are a negro!* If we call to our aid the thunder tones of the cannon and the arguments of fire arms, (vigorously managed by black and white men, side by side,) as displayed upon Dorchester Heights, and at Lexington, and at White Plains, and at Kingston, and at Long Island, and elsewhere, the retort is, *you are a negro*—if we present to the nation a Bunker's Hill, our nation's altar, (upon which she offered her choicest sacrifice,) with our fathers, and brothers, and sons, prostrate thereon, wrapped in fire and smoke—the incense of blood borne upward upon the wings of sulphurous vapor, to the throne of national honor, with a halo of national glory echoing back, and spreading and astonishing the civilized world;—and if we present the thousands of widows and orphans, whose only earthly protectors were thus sacrificed, weeping over the fate of the departed; and anon, tears of blood are extorted, on learning that the government for which their lovers and sires had died, refuses to be their protector;—if we tell that angels weep in pity, and that God, the eternal Judge, 'will hear the desire of the humble, judge the fatherless and the oppressed, that the man of the earth may no more oppress,'—the retort is, YOU ARE A NEGRO! If there is a spark of honesty, patriotism, or religion, in the heart or the source from whence such refuting arguments emanate, the devil incarnate is the brightest seraph in paradise.

CHAPTER III.

On the Nature of the Prejudice of the White Population of the United States, in Its Malignant Exercise towards the Colored People.

MALIGNANT prejudice is a principle which calls into action the worst passions of the human heart. There are cases, however, in which the exercise of prejudice is perfectly harmless. A person may prepossess favorable opinions of another, and such opinions may be just and right. Unfavorable opinions may be formed, also, of persons whose conduct is censurable; and a just prejudice may be exercised towards them, as they stand related to their own bad conduct, without a display of any malignity.

Again, prejudicial feelings may be exercised towards another, through an error of judgment, for the want of means of knowing the true character of those against whom a prejudice is indulged; in which case, it possesses nothing malignant, because its possessor entertains no purpose of injury. Great caution should be exercised, however, in judging the motives and conduct of another, especially when such conduct relates somewhat to ourselves—because it is very natural for us to be governed by our interest, or imaginary interest, which is liable to lead us into errors of the worst kind. It is also natural, on being convicted of wrong, to plead ignorance. But such a plea will not always excuse the pleader in strict justice. For if the prejudiced person has the means of knowing, or if he has any doubt with regard to the justness of his opinions of his neighbors, and still neglects to use the means of informing himself, and to solve his doubts on the subject, but persists in the exercise of his prejudice, he is equally guilty of all the mischief produced thereby, as he would be if he knew ever so well, and persisted in his wrong course in the light of that knowledge.

Prejudice seems to possess a nature peculiar to itself. It never possesses any vitiating qualities, except when it is exercised by one who has done, or intends to do, another an injury. And its malignity is heightened in proportion as its victim in any way recovers, or has a manifest prospect of recovering the injury; or if there is apparently a door open by which a superior power to that which he possesses, may bring him to an account for the wrong done to his neighbor, all have a direct tendency to heighten the malignity of prejudice in the heart of its possessor.

The colored population are the injured party. And the prejudice of the whites against them is in exact proportion to the injury the colored people have sustained. There is a prejudice in this country against the Irish, who are flocking here by thousands. Still there is nothing malignant in the nature and exercise of that prejudice, either national or personal. It grows out of the mere circumstance of their different manners and religion. The moment an Irishman adopts the maxims and prevailing religion of the country, he is no longer regarded an Irishman, other than by birth. It is to be remembered, also, that the Irish are not an injured, but a benefited party; therefore, it is not possible that the bestower of benefits could be at the same time malignantly exercising prejudice towards those he is benefiting.

There exists, therefore, no injurious prejudice against the Irish. There exists a prejudice against the Indians, but it is almost entirely national, and for the very reason that the injury they have sustained is essentially national. The jealous eye of this nation is fixed upon them as a nation, and has ever exercised the rigor of its prejudice towards them, in proportion as they attempted to recover their rightful possessions; or, in other words, just in proportion as the physical powers of the Indians, have dwindled to inefficiency, prejudice against them has become lax and passive. It revives only as they show signs of national life. The injury sustained by the colored people, is both national and personal; indeed, it is national in a twofold sense. In the first place, they are lineally stolen from their native country, and detained for centuries, in a strange land, as hewers of wood and drawers of water. In this situation, their blood, habits, minds, and bodies, have undergone such a change, as to cause them to lose all legal or natural relations to their mother country. They are no longer her children; therefore, they sustain the great injury of losing their country, their birthright, and are made aliens and illegitimates. Again, they sustain a national injury by being adopted subjects and citizens, and then being denied their citizenship, and the benefits derivable therefrom—accounted as aliens and outcasts, hence, are identified as belonging to no country—denied birthright in one, and had it stolen from them in another—and, I had like to have said, they had lost title to both worlds; for certainly they are denied all title in this, and almost all advantages to prepare for the next. In this light of the subject, they belong to no people, race, or nation; subjects of no government—citizens of no country—scattered surplus remnants of two races, and of different nations—severed into individuality—rendered a mass of broken fragments, thrown to and fro, by the boisterous passions of this and other ungodly nations. Such, in part, are the national injuries sustained by this miserable people.

I am aware that most people suppose the existence of color to be the cause of malignant prejudice. Upon this supposition an argument is founded, that color is an insurmountable barrier, over which there can be no social or political relation formed between white and colored Americans. To show the folly of which, I shall lay down and sustain the following principles.

First. Effects, according to their numerous laws, partake of their parent cause in nature and quantity; i.e. the amount of effect produced, will exactly agree with the amount of efficiency the cause contains which produced it; and their legitimacy claims for them, the nature of their parent. Apply this rule to the subject under consideration, and it will be seen, that, if color were the cause of prejudice, it follows, that just according to the variegation of the cause, (color) so would the effect variegate—i.e. the clear blooded black would be subject to a greater degree of prejudice, in proportion as he was black—and those of lighter caste subject to a less degree of prejudice, as they were light. Now it is well known that the exercise of prejudice, is as intense towards those who are in fact whiter than a clear blooded American, as it is against one who is as black as jet, if they are identified as belonging to that race of people who are the injured party.

Again. That which cannot be contemplated as a principle, abstractly, cannot be an efficient cause of any thing. A principle which is not subject to dissection, having body and parts—a principle of configuration is not capable of being an active cause; therefore, it only exists as a passive principle, depending entirely on an active principle for its existence. Now, if animal color can be contemplated as a cause, it must possess configurative properties; and if it possess these properties, then it is an independent principle, capable of living and acting after the man is dead, or decomposed. If it is argued that each component part of the man becomes independent when decomposed, and that animal color is one of the component parts, then I would ask, why we cannot comprehend its existence, the same as other matter of which the body was made? If this cannot be done, then it cannot be regarded other than a passive principle in which there is no power of action. Color, therefore, cannot be an efficient cause of the malignant prejudice of the whites against the blacks; it is only an imaginary cause at the most. It serves only as a trait by which a principle is identified.

The true cause of this prejudice is slavery. Slavery partakes of the nature and efficiency of all, and every thing, that is bad on earth and in hell. Its effect in the character of prejudice, as displayed towards the colored people, fully sustains my position—that effects partake of their parent cause, both in nature and quantity; for certainly, nothing short of every thing evil on earth and in hell, in the form and character of slavery could be capable of producing such prejudicial injuries, as those under which the colored people are doomed to suffer. It must be admitted, that slavery assumes a most vicious character in its exercise towards them. Never could a people exist under greater injuries, than those under which this people have existed in this country; slavery, in its worst form, is the cause of all injury sustained by them. The system of slavery in its effects, is imposed on the injured party in two forms, or by two methods. The first method is, by a code of laws, originating in public sentiment, as in slave states. The other is, prejudice originating in the same, as it exists in free states. The first method is prejudicial, and partakes of the corruptions of public sentiment, which is corrupted by prejudice; but prejudice, in that case, assumes the form of law, and, therefore, is not capable of inflicting such deep injuries, as when it exists without law. Because to all law there is a limitation, whether good or bad; hence, so far as the laws of slave states are concerned, a limitation of suffering may be contemplated, even under their direct influence. However severe slave laws may be, and however faithfully executed according to their letter and spirit—though by them the cup of injury be lavished out in full measure upon the objects of its abuse to the extent of its power, still, the innate principles of the human mind, will cause it to transcend such legal abuse, where a *limitation* can be comprehended.

Legal codes, however oppressive, have never as yet been able to crush the aspiring principles of human nature. The real monster slavery, cannot long exist, where it is sustained by legal codes only; it is forced to stand off, and is capable of imposing its shadow only, in comparison to what it is capable of doing by collateral aid. When public sentiment, therefore, has become so morally, civilly, and politically corrupted by the principles of slavery, as to be determined in crushing the objects of its malignity, it is under the necessity of calling prejudice to its aid, as an auxiliary to its adopted formal code of wickedness, clothed like a semi-devil, with all the innate principles of the old dragon himself. This auxiliary, is all powerfully capable of accommodating itself to local circumstances and conditions, and appearing with all the nature of the old beast, slavery; it is always ready to destroy every aspiration to civil, political and moral elevation, which arises in the breast of the oppressed. There is no pretext too absurd, by which to justify the expenditures of its soul-and-body-destroying energies. The complexion, features, pedigree, customs, and even the attributes and purposes of God, are made available to its justification.

By this monster, the withering influence of slavery is directed to the very vitals of the colored people—withering every incentive to improvement—rendering passive all the faculties of the intellect—subjecting the soul to a morbid state of insensibility—destroying the body—making one universal wreck of the best work of nature's God.

Such is its effect at the south, and scarcely less destructive at the north. The only difference is this: at the north, there is not so formal a code of laws by which to direct the energies of prejudice as at the south; still the doctrine of *expediency* full well makes up the deficiency of cruel laws, giving prejudice as full toleration to exercise itself, and in lavishing out its withering influence, as law at the south.

It is a remarkable fact that the moment the colored people show signs of life—any indication of being possessed with redeeming principles, that moment an unrelenting hatred arises in the mind which is inhabited by that foul fiend, prejudice; and the possessor of it will never be satisfied, until those indications are destroyed; space, time, nor circumstance, is no barrier to its exercise. Transplant the object of its malignity to Africa, or Canada, or elsewhere, and its poison is immediately transferred from local into national policy, and will exert all possible means it possesses, to accomplish its fell design. It always aims its deadly fangs at the noble and active principles of the immortal mind, which alone enables man to stand forth pre-eminent in all the works of God.*

Let the oppressed assume the character of capable men in business, either mercantile, mechanical, or agricultural,—let them assume the right of exercising themselves in the use of the common

*Take Hayti for an example.

privileges of the country—let them claim the right of enjoying liberty, in the general acceptation of the term—let them exercise the right of speech and of thought—let them presume to enjoy the privileges of the sanctuary and the Bible, let their souls be filled with glory and of God, and wish to bow the knee at the sacred altar, and commemorate the dying love of Christ the Lord—let them seek a decent burial for their departed friend in the church yard—and they are immediately made to feel that they are as a carcass destined to be preyed upon by the eagles of persecution. Thus they are followed from life's dawn to death's-doom.

I have no language wherewith to give slavery, and its auxiliaries, an adequate description, as an efficient cause of the miseries it is capable of producing. It seems to possess a kind of omnipresence. It follows its victims in every avenue of life.

The principle assumes still another feature equally destructive. It makes the colored people subserve almost every foul purpose imaginable. Negro or nigger, is an opprobrious term, employed to impose contempt upon them as an inferior race, and also to express their deformity of person. Nigger lips, nigger shins, and nigger heels, are phrases universally common among the juvenile class of society, and full well understood by them; they are early learned to think of these expressions, as they are intended to apply to colored people, and as being expressive or descriptive of the odious qualities of their mind and body. These impressions received by the young, grow with their growth, and strengthen with their strength. The term in itself, would be perfectly harmless, were it used only to distinguish one class of society from another; but it is not used with that intent; the practical definition is quite different in England to what it is here, for here, it flows from the fountain of purpose to injure. It is this baneful seed which is sown in the tender soil of youthful minds, and there culti- vated by the hand of a corrupt immoral policy.

The universality of this kind of education is well known to the observing. Children in infancy receive oral instruction from the nurse. The first lessons given are, Johnny, Billy, Mary, Sally, (or whatever the name may be,) go to sleep, if you don't the old *nigger* will carry you off; don't you cry—Hark; the old *nigger*'s coming—how ugly you are, you are worse than a little *nigger*. This is a specimen of the first lessons given.

The second is generally given in the domestic circle; in some families it is almost the only method of correcting their children. To inspire their half grown misses and masters to improvement, they are told that if they do this or that, or if they do thus and so, they will be poor or ignorant as a *nigger;* or that they will be black as a *nigger;* or have no more credit than a *nigger;* that they will have hair, lips, feet, or something of the kind, like a *nigger.* If doubt is entertained by any, as to the truth of what I write, let them travel twenty miles in any direction in this country, especially in the free States, and his own sense of hearing will convince him of its reality.

See nigger's thick lips—see his flat nose—nigger eye shine—that slick looking nigger—nigger, where you get so much coat?—that's a nigger priest—are sounds emanating from little urchins of Christian villagers, which continually infest the feelings of colored travellers, like the pestiferous breath of young devils; and full grown persons, and sometimes professors of religion, are not unfrequently heard to join in the concert.

A third mode of this kind of instruction is not altogether oral. Higher classes are frequently instructed in school rooms by referring them to the nigger-seat, and are sometimes threatened with being made to sit with the niggers, if they do not behave.

The same or similar use is made of nigger pews or seats in meeting-houses. Professing Christians, where these seats exist, make them a test by which to ascertain the amount of their humility. This I infer from their own language; for, say they, of the colored people, if we are only humble enough, we should be willing to sit any where to hear the word. If our hearts were right we should not care where we sit—I had as lief sit there (meaning the nigger pew,) as any where in the world. This, I admit, is all very good, but comes with rather bad grace. But, as I above observed, this kind of education is not altogether oral. Cuts and placards descriptive of the negroe's deformity, are every where displayed to the observation of the young, with corresponding broken lingo, the very character of which is marked with design. Many of the popular book stores, in commercial towns and cities, have their show-windows lined with them. The bar-rooms of the most popular public houses in the country, sometimes have their ceiling literally covered with them. This display of American civility is under the daily observation of every class of society, even in New England. But this kind of education is not only systematized, but legalized. At the south, public newspapers are teeming through the country, bearing negro cuts, with remarks corresponding to the object for which they are inserted.

But this system is not carried on without deep design. It has hitherto been a settled opinion of philosophers that a black man could endure the heat better than a white man. Traders in human flesh have ever taken the advantage of that opinion, by urging it as a plea of justification of their obtaining Africans, as laborers in warm climates; hence, we may naturally expect, that in a slave country like this, it would be a universally admitted axiom; and the more readily admitted, as it is easily construed into a plea to justify their wicked purposes. If the black can endure the heat, and the white cannot, say they, it must be that God made him on purpose for that; hence, it is no harm for us to act in accordance with the purposes of God, and make him work. These are the simple inferences drawn from the philosophical premises, the justness of which I shall hereafter examine.

The arguments founded on these premises, are many. Cotton, rice, indigo, tobacco, and sugar, are great blessings to the world, say they, and they may as well be made to make them as not; for they are a lazy crew at the best, and if they are not made to work for us, they will not work at all, &c. But to come at the truth, the whole system is founded in avarice. I believe the premises to be the production of modern philosophy, bearing date with European slavery; and it has been the almost sole cause of the present prevailing public sentiment in regard to the colored population. It has given rise to the universal habit of thinking that they were made for the sole end of being slaves and underlings. There could be nothing more natural, than for a slaveholding nation to indulge in a train of thoughts and conclusions that favored their idol, slavery. It becomes the interest of all parties, not excepting the clergy, to sanction the premises, and draw the conclusions, and hence, to teach the rising generation. What could accord better with the objects of this nation in reference to blacks, than to teach their little ones that a negro is part monkey?

'The love of money is the root of all evil'; it will induce its votaries to teach lessons to their little babes, which only fits them for the destroyers of their species in this world, and for the torments of hell in the world to come. When clergymen, even, are so blinded by the god of this world, as to witness the practice of the most heinous blasphemy in the house, said to be dedicated to God, for centuries, without raising their warning voice to the wicked, it would not be at all surprising if they were to teach their children a few lessons in the science of anatomy, for the object of making them understand that a negro is not like a white man, instead of teaching them his catechism.

The effect of this instruction is most disastrous upon the mind of the community; having been instructed from youth to look upon a black man in no other light than a slave, and having associated with that idea the low calling of a slave, they cannot look upon him in any other light. If he should chance to be found in any other sphere of action than that of a slave, he magnifies to a monster of wonderful dimensions, so large that they cannot be made to believe that he is a man and a brother. Neither can they be made to believe it would be safe to admit him into stages, steam-boat cabins, and tavern dining-rooms; and not even into meeting-houses, unless he have a place prepared on purpose. Mechanical shops, stores, and school rooms, are all too small for his entrance as a man; if he be a slave, his corporeality becomes so diminished as to admit him into ladies' parlors, and into small private carriages, and elsewhere, without being disgustful on account of his deformity, or without producing any other discomfiture. Thus prejudice seems to possess a magical power, by which it makes a being appear most odious one moment, and the next, beautiful—at one moment too large to be on board a steam-boat, the next, so small as to be convenient almost any where.

But prejudice is destructive to life. The public have been frequently told the operation of the slave system is destructive to the life of its victim; this statement is intended generally to be confined to those parts where slavery is legalized; and what has been said relative to the subject is but a beginning of the story. Indeed, I may say the publishers of the horrible effects of slavery in this country, have not generally had the means of knowing one half of its enormity. The extent of it will probably remain a secret until the great day of eternity. Many of us who are conversant with fugitive slaves, on their arrival to the free states, have an opportunity of hearing a tale of woe, which for the want of adequate language, we are not able to describe. These stories are told with so much native simplicity as to defy the most stubborn incredulity of the incredulous. But, though slavery in this way is carrying its thousands into eternity, in the southern states, yet it is doing hardly less so in the free states, as it displays itself in the character and form of prejudice.

Mind acts on matter. Contemplate the numerous free people of color under the despotic reign of prejudice—contemplate a young man in the ardor of youth, blessed with a mind as prolific as the air, aspiring to eminence and worth—contemplate his first early hopes blasted by the frost of prejudice—witness the ardor of youth inspiring him to a second and third trial, and as often repelled by this monster foe—hear him appealing to the laws of the land of his birth for protection—the haughty executives of the law spurning him from the halls of justice. He betakes to the temple of God—the last alternative around which his fading, dying hopes are hovering—but here, also, he receives a death thrust, and that by the hand of the priest of the altar of God. Yes—hear ye priests of the altar—it is the death thrust of slavery carried to the hearts of its victims by you. Yes—let it be known to the world, that the colored people who have been stolen, and have lost all allegiance to Africa, are sold in the shambles, and scouted from every privilege that makes life desirable. Under these discouragements they betake themselves to those who are called to preach good tidings to the meek, to bind up the broken-hearted, to proclaim liberty to the captives, and the opening of the prison doors to them that are bound, and they are set at nought by them also. The effect of these discouragements are every where manifest among the colored people.

I will venture to say, from my own experience and observation, that hundreds of them come to an untimely grave, by no other disease than that occasioned by oppression. And why should it be otherwise? They are virtually denied all possessions on earth, and how can they stay without a place whereon to rest.

I, as an individual, have had sufficient opportunity to know something about prejudice, and its destructive effects. At an early period of my life, I was extensively engaged in mechanism, associated with a number of other colored men of master spirits and great minds. The enterprise was followed for about twenty years, perseveringly, in direct opposition to public sentiment, and the tide of popular prejudice. So intent were the parties in carrying out the principles of intelligent, active free men, that they sacrificed every thing of comfort and ease to the object. The most rigid economy was adhered to at home and abroad. A regular school was established for the instruction of the youth connected with the factory, and the strictest rules of morality were supported with surprising assiduity; and ardent spirits found no place in the establishment. After the expenditure of this vast labor and time, together with many thousand dollars, the enterprise ended in a total failure. By reason of the repeated surges of the tide of prejudice, the establishment, like a ship in a boisterous hurricane at sea, went beneath its waves, richly laden, well manned, and well managed, and all sunk to rise no more. Such was the interest felt by the parties concerned, and such was their sense of the need of such an establishment for the benefit of colored youth, that they might acquire trades and a corresponding education, that they exerted every nerve to call it into the notice of the public, that the professed friends of the colored people might have an opportunity to save it from becoming a wreck; but all in vain; prejudice had decreed its fate. It fell, and with it fell the hearts of several of its undertakers in despair, and their bodies into their graves.

With the above, I could record the names of scores whose dissolution can be traced to a cloud of obstructions thrown in their way to prevent enterprise.

I should proceed no farther with this tale of woe, were I satisfied I had done my duty in the case. But the condition of the colored people is such, even in the free states, that every effort, however feeble, should be made to redeem them from the influence of that dreadful monster—prejudice. I have recently travelled among them as a missionary, and their condition is truly lamentable. Their immortal interests, as well as their temporal, are in many places almost entirely disregarded; and in others, their warmest friends seem not to comprehend their true condition. I found several hundreds in some places, who, though the bowl of knowledge was overflowing around them, were not permitted to partake, without they receive it from the cup of contempt, the thought of which, to sensitive minds, is like a draught of wormwood and gall.

Slavery, in the form and character of prejudice, is as fatal, yea, more fatal than the pestilence. It possesses imperial dominion over its votaries and victims. It demands and receives homage from priests and people. It drinks up the spirit of the church, and gathers blackness, and darkness, and death, around her brow. Its poison chills the life blood of her heart. Its gigantic tread on the Sabbath day, pollutes the altars of the sanctuary of the Most High. It withholds the word of life from thousands of perishing immortals, and shuts the gate of heaven alike upon those whose hearts it possesses, and those marked out for its victims. It opens wide the way to hell; and as though possessed with more than magic power, coerces its millions down to the pit of woe in defiance of the benevolence of a God, and the dying groans of a Saviour. O Prejudice, thou art slavery in disguise! and couldst thou ascend to heaven, thy pestiferous breath would darken and poison that now healthful and happy clime; and thou wouldst make its inhabitants feel the pains of the lowest hell. If there are degrees of intensity to the misery of the damned, that being must feel it in eternity, in whose heart prejudice reigned in this world. O Prejudice, I cannot let thee pass without telling thee and thy possessors, that thou art a compound of all evil—of all the corrupt passions of the heart. Yea, thou art a participant in all the purposes of the wicked one—thou art the very essence of hell.

CHAPTER IV.

On the Claims of the Colored People to all the Civil, Religious, and Social Privileges of this Country.

THIS PROPOSITION is in part embraced within the province of those of a preceding chapter. In following it, therefore, I shall be able to fulfill a promise therein contained.

The claims set up are founded in the fact that they are Americans by birth and blood. Complexion has never been made the legal test of citizenship in any age of the world. It has been established generally by birth and blood, and by purchase, or by the ceding of a province or territory from one nation to another. But as they are denied those privileges principally on the ground of their complexion and blood, it shall be my business in this concluding chapter to show—that though their complexion is as truly American as the complexion of the whites, yet it has nothing to do in settling the question. If blood has any thing to do with it, then we are able to prove that there is not a drop of African blood, according to the general acceptation of the term, flowing in the veins of an American born child, though black as jet. Children of African parents, recently arrived in this country, who have not undergone what is called seasoning, may partake of the characteristics of its African parents; such as the hair, complexion, and such like appendages, but the child's blood has nothing African about it, and for the following reasons. The blood of the parents in seasoning to this climate becomes changed—also, the food of the mother being the production of this country, and congenial to the climate—the atmosphere she breathes—the surrounding objects which strike her senses—all are principles which establish and give character to the constitutional principles of the child, among which the blood is an essential constituent; hence every child born in America, even if it be as black as jet, is American by birth and blood. The kind of root called Irish potatoes, is in truth American, if the potatoes are the production of American soil; and thus remain American potatoes, though they be red or deep scarlet. Some eagle-eyed philosophers, who possess great acuteness of smelling powers, think there is a difference of smell between the Africans and Europeans. Suppose that idea to be correct—would it prove any difference of smell between Americans who are constitutionally alike, and whose corporeals are sustained by the same ailment? In philosophically contemplating those constitutional properties, the color of the skin can no more be included than that of the eyes or the length of the nose.

It is the settled opinion of most people in this country, as I mentioned in a former chapter, that black Americans can endure the heat better than white Americans. This opinion is founded in the fact that black will retain heat while white emits it. I admit the proposition, but I doubt the correctness of the conclusions with respect to the color of animals.

Some minerals and dye-stuffs, and other black substances, will retain heat, which is owing to their not possessing any reflecting ingredient or property, by which the light or heat is thrown back. Heated iron will retain heat longer than heated brass, for the same reason—i.e. iron is not possessed of as much reflection as brass—or in other words, it has not the properties of reflection. I believe these are the considerations, and these only, that are capable of sustaining the proposition.

But these considerations do not and cannot embrace those connected with animal color, for that has neither the power of retaining nor emiting heat—and for the very good reason it possesses no properties; hence no efficient cause in itself to produce any effect whatever. The principle as it exists in relation to minerals and other substances, depends entirely upon the nature of the properties of which these several bodies are composed; but can the principle be made to apply to animal color?

Analyze black iron, and black properties are found in the iron. Analyze black dye-stuff, and black properties are found in the stuff. Analyze light brass, and light reflecting properties are found in the brass.

Analyze a black man, or anatomize him, and the result of research is the same as analyzing or anatomizing a white man. Before the dissecting knife passes half through the outer layer of the skin, it meets with the same solids and fluids, and from thence all the way through the body. Now I should like to have some modern philosophers, who have got more sense than common school-boys, to tell the world how it is that two bodies of matter, the one exactly similar to the other, in every minute principle of their composition, should produce different effect by the one emiting heat, and the other retaining it.

If it is contended that those properties exist in the animal color itself, then, if they will be good enough to analyze it and give us a knowledge of its parts—i.e. if they think a black head can receive and understand it—they will do the world a great favor, as well as ourselves.

If the foregoing considerations are reconcilable, then it may be taken for granted that a black man can work better in the hot sun than a white man—but if they are not reconcilable, then the whole theory is only calculated to dupe the black people, and make knaves of the white people.

But to return. The colored people being constitutionally Americans, they are depending on American climate, American aliment, American government, and American manners, to sustain their American bodies and minds; a withholding of the enjoyment of any American principle from an American man, either governmental, ecclesiastical, civil, social or alimental, is in effect taking away his means of subsistence; and consequently, taking away his life. Every ecclesiastical body which denies an American the privilege of participating in its benefits, becomes his murderer. Every state which denies an American a citizenship with all its benefits, denies him his life. Every community which denies an American the privilege of public conveyances, in common with all others, murders him by piece-meal. Every community which withholds social intercourse with an American, by which he may enjoy current information, becomes his murderer of the worst kind. The claims the colored people set up, therefore, are the claims of an American.

They ask priests and people to withhold no longer their inalienable rights to seek happiness in the sanctuary of God, at the same time and place that other Americans seek happiness. They ask statesmen to open the way whereby they, in common with other Americans, may aspire to honor and worth as statesmen—to place their names with other Americans—subject to a draft as jurymen and other functionary appointments, according to their ability. They ask their white American brethren to think of them and treat them as American citizens, and neighbors, and as members of the same American family. They urge their claims in full assurance of their being founded in immutable justice. They urge them from a sense of patriotism, from an interest they feel in the well being of their common country. And lastly, they urge them from the conviction that God, the judge of all men, will avenge them of their wrongs, unless their claims are speedily granted.

There are some objections urged against these claims. One is, that the greater part of the colored people are held as property, and if these claims are granted, their owners would be subject to great loss. In answer to this objection, I would remark, that were I to accede to the right of the master to his property in man, still I should conceive the objection groundless, for it is a well known fact that a far greater portion of the colored people who are free, purchased their freedom, and the freedom of their families. Many of them have purchased themselves several times over. Thousands of dollars have been paid over to masters annually, which was the proceeds of extra labor, in consideration of their expected freedom. My colored acquaintances are numerous who have thus done, some of whom were under the necessity of running away to obtain their freedom after all.

I am sufficiently acquainted with the sentiments and views of the slave population of every slave state in the union, to warrant me in the conclusion, that if the despotic power of the master was wrested from him, and the slaves placed under a law of ever so rigid a nature, with the privilege of paying for themselves by their extra labor, there would be comparatively few slaves in the country in less than seven years. The most of them would pay the round price of their bodies, and come out freemen.

Another objection is, that the slaves, if freed at once, would not be capable of enjoying suffrages.

This objection has less foundation than the former, for the several state legislatures of the slave states are continually assisting the masters to keep them in ignorance, and why not legislate in favor of their being informed?

Some contend that they are not now fit for freedom, but ought to be prepared and then freed.

Such a calculation is preposterous. We might as well talk about educating a water machine to run against its propelling power, as to talk about educating a slave for a free man. When travelling through the state of New York, recently, I made some inquiries with respect to the colored people, who in some places are very numerous. I was there informed, by gentlemen whose veracity I cannot doubt, that they are generally indolent and dissipated, far worse than they were when they were slaves. I was told also, that many of them had enjoyed excellent opportunities to become wealthy and respectable. That before the Emancipation Bill was passed in that state, they were mostly slaves, but had an opportunity of obtaining an excellent education, and the art of farming, equal, and in many instances, superior to most white men. When they became free, many of their masters, as a reward of former faithfulness, furnished them with means to operate for themselves on a small scale. My informants expressed much astonishment at the fact that most of those who had the best opportunity to do well, had become dissipated, and much worse in character and conduct than when they were slaves.

I have introduced this narrative for the purpose of showing that slaves cannot be educated for free men. A slave is metamorphosed into a machine, adapted to a specific operation, and propelled by the despotic power of the slave system, without any motive to attract. The influence of this power acts upon a slave the same as upon any other biased agent. By the abrogation of the propelling cause of all the acts of the machine, it ceases to move. The slave is now left, without either motive to attract, or power to coerce. A slave, as such, in undergoing the change from a moral, intelligent being, to a mere machine, lost all the innate principles of a freeman. Hence, when the principles of slavery ceases to act upon him, to the end for which he is a slave, he is left a mere out-of-use wreck of machinery; under nothing but the withering influence of the pelting rain of wickedness.

It is true, many of the slaves of New York had some education, but that education was acquired when a slave. Hence, it was only a collateral means by which he was rendered a more efficient machine. His education was the education of a slave, and not a freeman.

These conclusions may be thought by some to go against the doctrine of immediate abolition—not so. The doctrine of immediate abolition embraces the idea of an entire reversal of the system of slavery. The work of emancipation is not complete when it only cuts off some of the most prominent limbs of slavery, such as destroying the despotic power of the master, and the laying by of the cow-hide. The man who fell among thieves was emancipated in that way. His cruel captivators, I suppose, thought they had done a great act of philanthropy when they left off beating him. But their sort of emancipation left the poor man half dead—precisely in the same way New York emancipated her slaves, after beating them several hundred years, left them, half dead, without proscribing any healing remedy for the bruises and wounds received by their maltreatment. But the good Samaritan had quite a different view of the subject. It is remembered, undoubtedly, that before he acted, there were several who passed by that way, saw the man, but passed by on the other side. Whether they were Unionists, Colonizationists, or Abolitionists, every one must judge for themselves. But when the good man came along, he carried out the principles of immediate abolitionism. If New York had imitated him, there would have been no complaint about her emancipated negroes (as they are called,) being worse than when they were slaves.

I repeat, that emancipation embraces the idea that the emancipated must be placed back where slavery found them, and restore to them all that slavery has taken away from them. Merely to cease beating the colored people, and leave them in their gore, and call it emancipation, is nonsense. Nothing short of an entire reversal of the slave system in theory and practice—in general and in particular—will ever accomplish the work of redeeming the colored people of this country from their present condition.

Let the country, then, no longer act the part of the thief. Let the free states no longer act the part of them who passed by on the other side, and leaving the colored people half dead, especially when they were beaten by their own hands, and so call it emancipation—raising a wonderment why the half dead people do not heal themselves. Let them rather act the part of the good Samaritan. That only will open an effectual door through which sympathies can flow, and by which a reciprocity of sentiment and interest can take place—a proper knowledge acquired by the benefactor relative to his duty, and reciprocated on the part of the benefited.

This state of things would possess redeeming power. Every collateral means would be marshaled under the heaven-born principle, that requires all men to do unto others as they would that others should do unto them. It would kindle anew the innate principles of moral, civil and social manhood, in the downtrodden colored Americans; bidding them arise as from the dead, and speed their way back to the height from whence they have fallen. Nor would the call be in vain. A corresponding action on their part would respond to the cheering voice. The countenance which has been cast down, hitherto, would brighten up with joy. Their narrow foreheads, which have hitherto been contracted for the want of mental exercise, would begin to broaden. Their eye balls, hitherto strained out to prominence by a frenzy excited by the flourish of the whip, would fall back under a thick foliage of curly eyebrows, indicative of deep penetrating thought. Those muscles, which have hitherto been distended by grief and weeping, would become contracted to an acuteness, corresponding to that acuteness of perception with which business men are blessed. That interior region, the dwelling place of the soul, would be lighted up with the fires of love and gratitude to their benefactors on earth, and to their great Benefactor above, driving back those clouds of slavery and of prejudice which have hitherto darkened and destroyed its vision. And thus their whole man would be redeemed, rendering them fit for the associates of their fellow men in this life, and for the associates of angels in the world to come.

> Sons of Columbia, up get ye;
> Purge you from slavery's guilty stain,
> Defend the honest poor, the truth maintain.
>
> Sons of pilgrim sires, up get ye;
> Purge you from slavery's guilty stain,
> Your country's stained with blood all o'er the main.
>
> Priests of the altar, up get ye;
> Purge you from slavery's guilty stain,
> Cease to be slavery's vassals—dupes to gain.
>
> Priests of the altar up get ye;
> Purge you from slavery's guilty stain,
> No more the holy name of God profane.
>
> Priests of the altar, up get ye;
> Purge you from slavery's guilty stain,
> Come ye from under slavery's prejudicial reign.
>
> Priests of the altar, up get ye;
> Purge you from slavery's guilty stain,
> The trump of God has sounded—Hark—it sounds again.

The Claims of the Colored People

Daughters of freedom, up get ye;
Purge you from slavery's guilty stain,
Shall violated chastity call for help in vain?

Daughters of freedom, up get ye;
Purge you from slavery's guilty stain,
Ere thy sisters' grief 'gainst thee in heaven complain.

Statesmen of Columbia, up get ye;
Hark! Jefferson presuag'd from first,
Trembling for his country—proclaimed—God is just!!

Priests and people, all, up get ye;
Hark! hear the prophets tell,
How nations forgetting God are sent to hell.

Priests and people, all, up get ye;
Purge you from that dreadful sin,
Prejudice—of dev'lish extract—hellish fiend.

Priests and people, all, up get ye;
Repent ye while you may,
An awful judgment is at hand—God's vengeful day.

☞ The sermon, as proposed in our title page, is omitted on the account that it would swell the work far beyond our calculation. It will accompany a work entitled Easton's Lectures on Civil, Social, and Moral Economy, which will be presented to the public in a few weeks. The surplus proceeds of that work, as well as of this, after their expenses are paid, will be given to a colored society in Hartford, Con., who have lost their meeting-house by fire.

An extensive supply of this work may be had by forwarding an order to Isaac Knapp's Book Store and Liberator Office, No. 25 Cornhill. . . .

Wherein the works are deficient in their claims to patronage, it is

[The sermon that originally was to have accompanied Easton's *Treatise* but was promised instead for later publication has not been found, nor have the "Lectures on Civil, Social, and Moral Economy." The references to these additional writings, however, suggest that Easton had developed an even more ambitious agenda as moral critic and social analyst than the *Treatise* was able to express. It is unfortunate that we do not know what these works contain, or even if they were ever published. The additional pity, of course, is that Easton's death in 1837 allows us only to imagine what direction his thought might have taken in the future.

The list of "errata" on the final page suggests the enormous pains Easton took just as the *Treatise* was going to press to present his ideas with absolute precision and to correct even the smallest errors. Both his intellectual integrity and personal dignity as a "colored man" are revealed even in this final section. Eds.]

hoped will be made up by the claims of the suffering society, for whom the proceeds are intended.

ERRATA.

6th page, 6th line from the top, instead of 'sprung' read 'springing'—and for 'you may find' read 'are found.'

10th page, 2d paragraph, 6th line, instead of 'conquest of armies' read 'conquest in arms'—also, 3d paragraph, 6th line, instead of 'impossible' read 'improbable.'

11th page, 1st line, instead of 'learning' read 'litany.'

12th page, 3d line, instead of 'by conveyance' read 'by *other* conveyance,'—also, instead of 'kindred and' &c. read 'subjects or' &c.—and for 'defender' read 'defendants.'

14th page, last paragraph, 2d line, instead of 'have annual,' &c. read 'receive annual,' &c.

18th page, 3d paragraph, 5th line, instead of 'the superiority' read 'the *pretended* superiority.'

19th page, 9th line from the top, read after 'and,' '*their country*' virtually, &c.

24th page, 2d paragraph, two last lines, instead of 'their progenitors since that period,' read 'since the commencement of that period.'

26th page, 2d paragraph, 12th line, instead of 'pangs' read 'fangs.'

28th page, 3d, 4th, 5th and 6th lines from the bottom, read thus: 'In convoking the Continental Congress of the 4th of September, 1774, there was not a word said about color. At a subsequent period, Congress met again, and agreed to get in readiness 12,000 men, to act in any emergency; also, a request was' &c.

31st page, 4th paragraph, 1st line, instead of 'Moble' read 'Mobile.'

34th page, 7th line from the top, for 'halo' read 'halloo.'

45th page, 5th line from the top, instead of 'surprising' read 'unsurpassing.'